THE
QUALITY
MASTER PLAN

THE
QUALITY
MASTER PLAN

A QUALITY STRATEGY FOR
BUSINESS LEADERSHIP

J.P. RUSSELL

THE QUALITY MASTER PLAN

A Quality Strategy for Business Leadership

J.P. Russell

Library of Congress Cataloging-in-Publication Data

Russell, J.P. (James P.)
     The quality master plan : a quality strategy for business
  leadership / J.P. Russell.
        p.   cm.
     Includes bibliographical references.
     ISBN 0-87389-081-7
     1. Quality control. 2. Production management — Quality control.
  I. Title.
  TS156.R87 1990
  658.5'62—dc20   89-18026
                                                              CIP

Copyright © 1990 by ASQC Quality Press

10987654321

ISBN 0-87389-081-7

Acquisitions Editor: Jeanine L. Lau
Production Editor: Tammy Griffin
Cover design by Wayne Dober. Set in Eras by DanTon Typographers.
Printed and bound by Edwards Brothers.

Printed in the United States of America

ASQC Quality Press, American Society for Quality Control
310 West Wisconsin Avenue, Milwaukee, Wisconsin 53203

TABLE OF CONTENTS

PREFACE

This book is dedicated to every CEO, manager, supervisor, and employee who has had the initiative and judgment to implement the quality improvement process for a new way of doing business that leads to growth and prosperity.

The Quality Master Plan presents a practical, step-by-step business plan for the implementation of the quality improvement process. It is designed to be user friendly in both format and terminology; it is based on actual experience in implementing the quality process in the workplace, and it encompasses information from quality consultants and academic sources.

This book was developed to fill a perceived need of CEOs, owners, managers, and professionals of all size businesses: the need for guidance in executing the theoretical principles of quality into the reality of day-to-day business. Its aim is to provide an insightful common sense plan for achieving total quality management.

In November of 1982, *Business Week* reported that "many experts believe the prestige of U.S.-made products could be restored by the end of this decade." The decade is drawing to a close, yet much remains to be accomplished in implementing continuous quality improvement for U.S. business.

In presenting *The Quality Master Plan,* I have avoided the coining of new phrases and terms which may lead to separation of the quality program from the rest of the business. The book is written to make

The Quality Master Plan presents a practical, step-by-step business plan for the implementation of the quality improvement process.

common business sense and is not a collection of theories. Further assistance is provided in the form of a "help" section which has examples pertinent to the plan. A glossary lists the terms generally used to describe the quality system.

Section III — Help of *The Quality Master Plan* includes example action item lists, problem-solving and supplier qualification sections, customer complaint categories and types, and a quality plan schedule. The schedule is displayed on a Gantt chart which lists the goals, strategies, and activities, resources, levels of effort, and timing. The Gantt chart is not a rigorous application of scheduling for any particular organization but provides an overview of the activities and timing relative to reasonable resource limitations. "Quality milestones" are significant, clear-cut accomplishments in the quality improvement process and are noted throughout the text.

The Quality Master Plan is a result of working from the inside of organizations and practicing the theories and principles of the quality improvement process from the shop floor to the management suite. All the examples are based on actual situations, although fictitious names have been used to prevent recognition of any company or person.

ACKNOWLEDGMENTS

I would like to thank several exceptional friends in the business community who shared their enthusiasm on the subject of quality. Whether it was reviewing the manuscript or sharing ideas, their encouragement provided nourishment as I traveled along the quality highway. I would like to extend personal gratitude to my wife, Jan, for endless hours of reviewing and correcting. Her understanding and support provided the time window for this contribution. A special acknowledgment to my children, Paul and Rachel, for their acceptance and trust of my decision to undertake the development of this work and for the use of their names in the examples.

To my development editor, Lillian Rodberg, I would like to acknowledge her guidance and interest beyond normal review and editorial comments.

I firmly believe that the undefined special efforts and value-added inputs from the above individuals are responsible for transforming the ordinary to the extraordinary.

SECTION I
INTRODUCTION

QUALITY: WHO NEEDS IT?

The U.S.A. for Business has formed a lottery to help businesses. You have just won a million dollars! As a leader in your organization, what problems would you want to solve? A recent Gallup survey reported that the top U.S. executives rated product and service quality as the most critical problems they face today. However, quality is not something that you can buy like a boat or automobile. It is not a machine that can be installed on the third floor. Nor does Japan have a monopoly on quality. Quality is a way of doing business regardless of the continent, language, or size of business.

The impact of quality is everywhere around us. Yet quality — also known as *goodness* and *general excellence* — has proven to be elusive. Consider the following companies, products, and services:

Singer	Sewing machines
Lionel	Electric trains
Greyhound	Bus service
Pullman	Rail cars
Chris Craft	Cabin cruisers

All these companies and their products were household words. Today, not one of these original companies is in the business that it pioneered.

In 1976, six U.S. banks ranked in the world's top 10; only one Japanese bank did. In 1986, seven Japanese banks ranked among the top 10; not a single U.S. bank did. The highest-ranking U.S. bank was 17th. In 1988, the Japanese asked why the United States has stewardship of the World Bank and the International Monetary Fund (IMF). They suggested that the dollar give way to a new international standard for currency. Perhaps the yen?

In the 1950s, "Made in Japan" was synonymous with "junk." Today it is synonymous with excellence. Americans are purchasing foreign automobiles (31 percent and climbing), foreign cameras, foreign TV sets, foreign tape recorders, and foreign VCRs. Now the Japanese are beginning to explore market demands for "soft" products like cosmetics.

The times they are a 'changing. U.S. manufacturers, once considered the best and most reliable in the world, are being phased out of more and more areas. Why? Because consumers perceive foreign products as having higher quality.

As someone in business, you realize this. Perhaps that realization or your competitive environment led you to read this book. Quality has become a popular theme. However, before setting out in pursuit of quality, we have to define it. Have you seen quality? Can you describe quality? But, as a teabag company's "tagline" says, "If you don't know what you want to do, it's harder to do it."

It's probably easier to start out with what quality isn't.

Quality Error #1:
Defining Quality by Company Standards

Every business manager and business owner is also a customer — both inside and outside his or her organization. When you're wearing your customer hat, how often do you encounter situations like the following?

- The mechanic says your car is fixed. You ransom it, retrieve it from the parking lot, and drive it home. You're no sooner on the highway than you hear the same grinding noise that made you take it for repair in the first place.
- You're on a business trip. Your breakfast home fries are burnt; your over easy eggs are over hard; your steak is well done instead of rare; all the food is cold except the orange juice, which is lukewarm.
- You're on your way to Chicago with a confirmed reservation. You're told the flight was overbooked and you've been put on standby. You're lucky — you do get a seat. But someone else's boarding pass has the same seat number. And when that's straightened out the plane sits on the runway for an hour and no one tells you why.
- It's Christmas Eve — or rather, 4 o'clock on Christmas morning. You've been up half the night trying to assemble your son's tape deck according to 20 pages of instructions written by a dyslexic sadist. To connect part A to part B you need locknut X. It's missing.

Certainly the suppliers of these products and services didn't set out to hassle their customers. All of them had quality standards of some kind. The auto shop has the newest repair manuals, a computerized parts system, and electronic diagnostics. The restaurant just won the Cleanliness Trophy for its chain. The airline has the best on-time record in the business. The tape deck meets the highest standards for signal-to-noise ratio, absence of "flutter," and concert-hall sound.

What's wrong here? Quality Error #1: Defining quality in terms of your goals instead of your customers' needs and wants. Standards and policies

4

were set by management without input from customers. As a customer yourself, don't you have one basic requirement that comes before all others? You want the product or service to work — *the first time.*

Example: On a business trip, I checked in a new, intact suit bag with Swiftair, Inc. What I checked out was a tangle of straps, torn fabric, white foam, and sticky green paste. I was able to identify the mangled remains because my name tag was on the amputated handle. Closer inspection revealed that all the straps had been cut, the high-strength, tear-resistant nylon was shredded in several places, and all my clothes were either torn or covered with a black, tar-like goo. The shaving cream can had exploded and the toothpaste tube had been smashed flat.

You might say that this mutilated suit bag did demonstrate excellence in its own way. If its objective was a search-and-destroy mission targeting my belongings, Swiftair's baggage-handling procedure was a complete success.

With the evidence in hand, I reported the crime to Swiftair. First, they wanted to inspect the suit bag to determine whether it could be repaired. Then I was subjected to a third-degree interrogation implying I was some kind of weirdo out to get a new suit bag at Swiftair's expense. Finally, I was reimbursed for the bag and its contents — but not for the time it took to pursue the complaint and to re-outfit myself. After all, Swiftair maintained, they handle so much luggage that something like this is bound to happen every once in a while.

Quality, we begin to see, consists of much more than meeting some set of standards some of the time. Quality consists of meeting the customer's expectations for that particular product or service. An airline may get you to your destination on time most of the time, but if you are bumped to another flight. . .if the plane sits on the runway for an unexplained hour. . .if your luggage looks as though it has gone through a paper shredder, then the airline is not meeting your expectations. You have not received quality for your money. The product or service did not meet your perceived needs.

> Quality, we begin to see, consists of much more than meeting some set of standards some of the time.

How do you feel about it? Unhappy? Angry? Cheated? Frustrated? You purchase a product or service because of an implied promise of expected value. You work hard; your time is valuable; you can't afford to waste time or money on products or services that don't do what they are supposed to do.

What will you do about it? Most likely, you'll switch to another supplier: You'll look for another garage to work on your car. . .try the service of another restaurant.

What happens to suppliers when a significant number of customers start switching? They lose money or go out of business. What happens to suppliers to whom the customers switch? They make money. In other words, quality pays. Lack of quality costs *you* money.

In the past, quality has been defined as a specified level of conformance to specifications or adherence to company procedures. This definition enables the manufacturer to say, "But sir, we are meeting every one of our performance level standards, which call for a 2 percent defect rate. We're sorry there were no whatzits in your tape recorder package — you just happened to receive one of our acceptable-defect units."

The fact is that specification tolerance levels don't produce quality because they imply that some level of poor performance is acceptable. Specifications are minimum requirements and may have little or no relationship to your customers' actual needs and wants. The tolerance level approach is self-defeating. No, you cannot realistically expect to achieve zero defects. But by striving for 100 percent performance — for getting it right the first time — you will come proportionately much closer than you will by setting some lower standard. For example, the U.S. Postal Service targets a 2 percent level of damaged packages. It manages to meet that performance level in the sense that it damages at least 2 percent of the packages it handles. Federal Express targets zero damage and in fact has a damage rate of less than 0.5 percent.

"Close enough is good enough" doesn't work and is too expensive. Doing it over — and over — wastes resources. American business cannot compete solving Problem #27 over and over again. To compete in today's global marketplace, we have to do it right the first time.

Nor is it sufficient to hoist the engineer's flag and define quality as "quality of design" or as using the most expensive components. In terms of "design quality," a Lincoln is considered better than a Ford, a Cadillac better than a Chevrolet. The designers of these automobiles defined quality in terms of costly premium features that promise greater comfort, appearance, or performance. "You get what you pay for" is the slogan. The more you pay, the better the quality — right?

I used to believe that myself. Then, a few years ago, I bought a "luxury" automobile:

- The clock didn't work.
- The electronic gas gauge registered a quarter tank when the tank was full.
- The hydraulic trunk lid lifters were too weak to support the lid's weight.
- The electronic seat adjustment for the passenger seat malfunctioned.
- The steering wheel wasn't aligned with the direction of the car.

Was I getting quality?

Now, what about the friend who bought the bottom-line Toyota for basic transportation and had no problems with the car for 89,000 miles? Which of us was getting quality?

Today, U.S. auto manufacturers are trying to rectify these problems. The hopeful sign is that they are trying to rectify them in terms of what the customer wants. In one program, customers are invited to return the car for a full refund if they find themselves not satisfied with it. In other words, the customer, not the automaker, defines quality.

Now, let's stop for a moment and review what quality *is not* to see whether we can arrive at what quality *is*:

- Quality is not a product or service internal specification.
- Quality is not some level of conformance to specifications.
- Quality is not the number of design features or a long list of services.
- Quality is not related to cost.

What is quality, then?

- For the customer, quality is getting what you were expecting.
- For the supplier, quality is getting it right the first time.

How do you find out what the customer expects or requires? Ask the customer — or, at the very least, put yourself in the customer's place.

An Experiment in Customer Expectations

Do you have a pen in your pocket or purse? Take it out. Hold it in your hand. Now, without looking at the box at the end of this chapter, start listing what you expect from your pen. What makes it a quality product in terms of your expectations?

Compare your expectations with those in the box (see page 12). How did you do? I'd guess that you didn't realize how many expectations you have for a simple writing tool.

Now ask a friend or associate to list his or her expectations. Compare them with yours. Are they the same?

There are two points to be made here. First, your pen is a quality product only to the extent that it meets your expectations. If the ink is indelible, but it leaks all over your clothes, the fact that the ink meets the manufacturer's standards for durability doesn't matter to you. If the pen is gold plated but skips when it writes, the fact that it's gold will just make you angrier about the skipping.

Second, beyond certain minimums, not everyone will have the same set of expectations for any product. A pen that doesn't write won't satisfy anyone, and neither will one that leaks. Beyond that, expectations will be individually defined. A 29¢ pen and a $29 pen can both be quality products.

Who defines quality in a product or service? Not the company manager or the quality control inspector, but the customer.

7

Quality Error #2: Shooting the Messenger

When you say "the customer is #1" does it end up being on "a Bo Derek scale"? Has your business become an expert at hassling customers who complain?

Customers who complain are your most valuable customers. Remember, most customers who have problems with your product won't bother to complain to you — they'll just go away mad and complain to their friends.

Customer complaints are signposts pointing out your road to better quality. But that's not how we always treat them.

- You go back to the mechanic with the grinding noise that wasn't fixed the first time. It takes two weeks to reschedule your repair. When you arrive to pick up the car, the service manager says: "We couldn't fix it. We don't have the part. Nah, we don't know when it'll come in. Call in a week and ask."
- You're moving. You turn in your telephone at the telephone center and buy a new one. You're billed for two telephones. You call and explain. The telephone company continues to hassle you. It takes months, endless photocopying, and the help of a local consumer hotline to make the company admit you returned a telephone. You think you've won. Then you get a notice that your "delinquent" account has been turned over to a collection agency.

You're #1? On what scale?

Is your company focusing on its internal convenience while the customer — the person who pays the bills and keeps you in business — is forgotten? When I went to the local shopping mall, I thought it was my bad luck that all the closest parking spaces were taken. Then I dropped off my daughter at her part-time job before the mall was open for customers. The parking places were already filled with cars belonging to mall personnel. The customers were relegated to the North 40 by the very people whose jobs depend on pleasing them.

If a customer dares to complain — that is, to express needs and expectations — what do you do? Many businesses have an attitude best expressed as "We are here to serve you — so long as you don't make waves."

The World Almanac and Book of Facts for 1988 reported that complaints about airline service doubled in the first six months of 1987 compared with the same period in 1986. The U.S. Department of Transportation was receiving complaints at the rate of 32,000 per year. Sixty percent involved flight delays, cancellations, or lost baggage. The transportation department believed these complaints represented only a fraction of actual incidents, since travelers are instructed to complain first to the airlines. The airlines' explanation: Complaints rose because the complaint system had received increased publicity.

This response totally sidesteps questions the airlines should be asking of themselves. Why are there so many complaints? What are we going to do about reducing the occurrence of problems? (Presumably, what they would like to do is keep the complaint system secret, thereby reducing the complaints, if not the problems.)

Customers are penalized for complaining: They are made to stand in line or languish on "hold"; they are treated as troublemakers; the seriousness of their complaints is sloughed off with "It was good enough for everyone else," or "Who do they think we are — Santa Claus?" or "They're always complaining!" or "We followed our procedures to the letter."

Now, consider how two different businesses responded to customer complaints.

Ms. M., a loyal customer, sent a pair of ill-fitting gloves back to the store where she bought them. In her letter, she mentioned that she had spent several hundred dollars at the shop and that this was the first time she had been disappointed in a purchase. She mentioned several aspects of the store's service that she liked and closed her letter with some suggestions for improvement.

The proprietor's reply:

> Dear Customer:
>
> I am in receipt of your letter of 5/5/89. I am sorry you found our store policies unsatisfactory. Our policies are clearly stated and also posted at the front desk. Once merchandise has left the store, we are no longer responsible. All transactions are final.
>
> Enclosed please find a check for $15.00 for the gloves you mailed back with your letter. I am issuing this refund because I find the whole matter petty and annoying. This should settle your dispute.

If you were Ms. M., would you patronize this store again?

In the second instance, a customer wrote to report being given substandard lodging when an airline's flight was cancelled owing to poor weather conditions. The customer asked nothing of the airline, simply stating that he wanted management to be aware of the problems he had experienced.

Dear Mr._____:

The disappointing events which prompted your letter about your trip are of serious concern to us. We can understand how upsetting this incident must have been and hope you will accept our sincere apology.

I share your disappointment that the hotel accommodations we provided were substandard. A copy of your comments has been forwarded to our General Manager in [city] so that we can handle similar situations in an improved manner.

As tangible evidence of our concern, a voucher is enclosed to encourage you to give us another opportunity to meet your travel needs. At this point, we ask that you use the voucher soon and give us the privilege of providing you with the high quality of service you deserve and we want to provide.

If you were the customer, would you give this airline a second chance? Neither business did it right the first time. But the business that acknowledges the importance of the customer and the validity of his or her concerns is the one that will probably have the opportunity to do it right the second time. As a matter of practice, companies that make zero defects their goal also do the best job of making up for such defects as they occur.

Customers may not expect 100 percent performance; they do — and are entitled to — expect 100 percent satisfaction.

To review: Quality is striving for 100 percent performance and achieving 100 percent customer satisfaction.

Quality Error #3: Quality Costs

If you approach quality as being 100 percent customer satisfaction, you'll find that quality does not cost — it pays. Customers reward businesses that supply quality goods and services. They penalize companies that don't.

Quality works to improve both ends of the balance sheet. It opens up new market opportunities and improves competitiveness by lowering your costs. Doing it wrong . . . doing it over . . . checking to ensure it is right . . . these are the costs of quality. Learning how to do it right the first time is how quality saves.

Quality pays: Every way, every day!

- *Quality pays off for your customers.* When customers receive products and services that consistently meet their needs, they can make full use of their resources. In the case of business customers, this means that they can better compete in the marketplace for growth and prosperity that benefits you as well as them.

Quality: Who needs it?. . . We all do.

- *Quality pays off for you as a customer of your suppliers* because getting materials and services that meet your needs and expectations eliminates waste and reduces your costs.
- *Quality pays off for your employees* not only because it ensures their jobs, but through better working relationships within your organization, of which each department is both a customer of and a supplier to other departments.
- *Quality pays for every U.S. consumer* by giving everyone what he or she pays for and eliminating the stress of endless hassles and frustrations.
- *Quality pays for every U.S. business* by making it possible to compete successfully in a rapidly changing global marketplace.

Knowing what quality consists of is the first step toward achieving it in your business. The answer to the question "Quality: Who needs it?" is "We all do."

Brainstorming: What makes a quality pen?

What do I expect of a pen?
What are its quality features?

- Style.
- It writes.
- It was free.
- It's gold/silver plated.
- It doesn't skip.
- It works every time.
- It's cheap; I lose pens all the time.
- It's durable.
- It has a brand name/prestige.
- It doesn't leak in my pocket or purse.
- The clip doesn't break easily.
- It's easy to hold, well-designed.
- It's disposable.
- It's not disposable.
- The ink lasts a long time.
- It retracts or extends as required.
- Replacement parts (i.e., cartridges) are easy to obtain.
- It's available at many outlets.
- The ink is the right color.
- The pen is the right color.
- The pen point is fine, medium, regular.

THE QUALITY MASTER PLAN: AN OVERVIEW

The quality master plan is the management system for the integration of quality principles and quality management tools into the organization. Just as quality must be built into a product or service, so must the quality process be built into the management structure and day-to-day activities.

The quality improvement process is a continuous, never-ending series of actions based on new business principles that will result in a competitive business and/or organization. The quality improvement process means everyone working together to consistently provide the best value to his or her customer(s).

The quality improvement process has the following advantages over other business projects or new ventures:

- It can be started with very little capital.
- It requires no previous experience or special expertise.
- It can be applied to any kind of business or organization.
- It will secure a competitive position and provide new market opportunities.
- It has a proven record of success.
- It has low business risk, yet high return.

As you read this book, note that every organization is capable of implementing the quality improvement process to meet its future competitive needs.

The business plan approach has been successful in operating businesses, therefore, it makes sense to use a business approach to implement quality improvement. *The Quality Master Plan* integrates quality principles into a sound business approach. Typically, publications on quality present a random laundry list of quality do's and don'ts and make no attempt to flange them into a business framework. In contrast, *The Quality Master Plan* applies business principles and uses examples and benefits based on actual situations.

This text presents principles and definitions of quality to overcome the limitations of the various closely held quality philosophies. In particular, the *quality triad* has been created to encompass the whole meaning and value of quality. The new problem-solving methods introduced here are simple, closely reflect reality, and meet the requirements for continued quality improvement. The suggested *customer CPR program* focuses attention on the customer and provides insight into future expectations and market opportunities.

The Quality Master Plan offers a preferred alternative to the trial-and-error method of implementation. The iterative approach — keep doing it until you get it right — is expensive and leads to poor use of resources. Quality improvement requires action to prevent problems before they occur. This text provides everything you need to set up the quality framework, initiate the process, and support the evolution of total quality management within the organization. It is a road map to quality improvement, complete with alternate routes, warnings, roadblocks, and caution areas.

The Quality Improvement Process

The quality improvement process is a management philosophy based on a definition of quality (the quality triad) and on principles of quality (the keys to quality). The quality improvement process consists of focusing on the system(s) that improve the way you make a product (or provide a service) to meet customer requirements and expectations and to provide maximum value.

The word "process" is used to describe all interactions and systems. A process can be any series of actions or operations that lead to a desired result. It is important to grasp that quality improvement is not a program in the traditional sense but transcends all programs and business initiatives. The quality improvement process is a way of doing business that will ultimately improve your bottom line.

The quality improvement process will: *goals.*

- Improve competitiveness.
- Eliminate waste and rework.
- Build customer confidence.
- Lead to growth and prosperity.

The foundations of *The Quality Master Plan* are quality concepts and a quantifiable definition of quality. Your organization must choose the definition that best fits your specific needs and focus. Your definition of quality should be consistent with your organization's quality policy and/or mission statement. Some companies have chosen to define quality in limited ways and thereby have limited their implementation of the quality improvement process.

Each of the many definitions of quality provide some insight as to what quality really is, but no single definition fits every situation. To define quality by a single criterion is like the blind men and the elephant. Each described a part of the elephant (the trunk, leg, tail, ears, side) but none was able to fully describe the animal. Similarly, the true definition of quality is greater than any of the popular definitions.

I have created the *quality triad* (Figure 1) to provide a universal definition that is flexible and applicable to all phases of a business operation.

Consistently providing the **customer** with products and services that:

- Conform to mutually agreed upon requirements.
- Strive to meet expectations.
- Maximize value (utility).

REQUIREMENTS

EXPECTATIONS

VALUE

Figure 1   The Quality Triad

The quality triad gives us the holistic focus for the existing businesses (conform to requirements), future opportunities (expectations), and the economic driving force (maximizing value or utility). Its components should be used to verify that your organization's outputs and deliverables conform to the customers' requirements, expectations, and value.

Conformance to mutually agreed upon customer requirements addresses existing product and service issues. Conformance to requirements of the customer is broader in scope than just meeting specifications. Specifications are often limited to the minimum market requirements for a product or service and may not reflect the customers' actual needs. In addition, specifications are narrowly focused on the product or service (e.g., percent activity, repair jobs completed, product within tolerances) and do not encompass parameters such as uniformity, consistency, timeliness, performance of product or service, or condition returned.

Striving to meet customer expectations opens the way to new market extensions and initiatives. A singular emphasis on requirements may create tunnel vision that blocks out the changing environment in the marketplace. Even those companies that consistently meet requirements can ill afford to sit back, relax, and close their eyes to the future. They, too, must look for new market opportunities defined by striving to meet customer expectations. It is such striving to meet expectations that has brought us automatic teller machines, express car rental check in, and convenience marts. Meeting expectations differentiates products (or services) and adds a dynamic characteristic to the quality improvement process.

Providing products or services that have the *maximum value or utility* is the economic driving force for the system of exchanging products and services. When used in this sense, *utility* refers to a fitness for some purpose or worth. The most basic requirement of a quality product or service is that the receiver will gain some benefit (monetary or personal) from purchasing and/or using the product or service. If the customer is to gain the *maximum* benefit, the product or service must be consistent in quality and must conform to the customer's expected value. In other words, if a product or service is not of consistently good quality or if it is out of specification, the customer will suffer economic injury due to process problems, poor performance of the finished product (loss of sales), rework costs, loss of productivity (doing it over), or increased appraisal costs (more inspection).

The Keys to Quality Improvement

Key #1: Continuous customer focus and satisfaction
Key #2: Total management commitment and support
Key #3: The building of trust and team spirit
Key #4: Implementation of systems for prevention, measurement, and elimination of problems

The first key to quality, *continuous customer focus and satisfaction,* sets a standard as well as a target for the organization. The organization must set its sights on the customer, both internally and externally. The standard is continuous (never-ending), 100 percent satisfaction. Just as the environment keeps changing, so do customer requirements and expectations. Every individual of an organization must design and produce products and services that provide the maximum value to the customer. Providing a product or service may require several steps, involving many people and functions. In every step there are customers and suppliers, each adding value, to meet the expectations of the final external customer.

The second key to quality, *total management commitment and support*, ensures that quality improvement is given the proper priority and that resources are available to implement the quality improvement process. Only management can change the way business is conducted. Only management, from the very top person on down, can change the culture of the organization. Only management can set the priorities and ensure that the resources are available to implement the process. The commitment must be reflected in everything that management says and does. The "how to" of management commitment is discussed in the remainder of this book.

The third key, *the building of trust and team spirit*, is the catalyst or activator of the quality improvement process. Trust cannot be mandated, but it is one of the building blocks for empowering managers and employees to correct every defect and nonconformance. Everything we do involves some level of trust — sitting on a chair, crossing a bridge, purchasing a product. Implicit in each action is the assurance that things will go as expected — the chair isn't broken, the bridge will support the vehicle, the product will perform. Without trust there would be perpetual fear, leading to total paralysis.

> Quality improvement is not inspecting quality after the fact, but building quality into the product or service.

The fourth and final key to quality, *implementation of systems for prevention, measurement, and elimination of problems*, provides the tools for continuous, never-ending quality improvement. Quality improvement is not inspecting quality after the fact, but building quality into the product or service. Quality management is proactive by preventing the errors and nonconformances, not reactive, by waiting and reacting to problems on a day-by-day/hour-by-hour basis.

The Quality Master Plan

The quality master plan is a business plan organized into a business format with a strategic objective, goals, strategies, and activities. Each strategy is explained by action steps and a discussion. By using this text you can implement quality philosophies into a practical application of the continuous quality improvement process. The quality master plan was developed from 20 years of experience in business and tested during six years of applying the quality process in the workplace. Actual business situations are used to show how each strategy and activity can be achieved.

The achievement of total quality management (continuous improvement) is not limited to specific tasks such as computer training skills or repair of equipment. Total quality management is an integral part of the way business is conducted — the decisions made every day. For example, purchasing a computer for the accounting department does not transform the department into an automated financial center. Training must be provided, software developed, systems restructured, and computer hardware/software purchased and installed. Once an organization has committed to the decision to automate the offices or operations, it has also committed to training, installation of the proper tools, and the cultural transformation that will be required for changing how the office or operation is managed. A decision to implement total quality (quality improvement process) requires the same type of commitment as any business investment or new initiative.

The quality master plan defines a business objective and lists goals for the organization (Figure 2). The strategies and steps supporting the goals will vary from company to company depending on each firm's environment and type of business. Your business should review the plan's strategies and steps to define what will best fit your individual situation, but remember that all strategies must be addressed even though the form and level of effort may differ.

The goals of the quality master plan were developed to be consistent with the basic quality principles of the quality improvement process. The four basic goals that support the business objective are:

- Integrate and promote quality management.
- Build an organization responsive to customer needs and wants.
- Consistently provide value to the customer.
- Achieve continuous improvement.

The first goal is to *integrate and promote quality management*. The keys to quality improvement that apply to this goal are:

Key #2: Total management commitment and support
Key #3: The building of trust and team spirit

To the purist, the word "promotion" may cause some difficulty. Experience in marketing has demonstrated the value of promotion as a tool for recognition of some idea, product, or service. However, promotion without substance or commitment is like a house of cards: One slip and the house will fall!

The second goal is to *build an organization responsive to customer needs and wants* (quality triad components). This goal deals with education in the quality process and structuring the organization for implementation. Each step and activity should be evaluated with consideration given to the specific

18

Objective: Change the organization culture (attitude) to a total quality way of management to improve competitiveness (survival) and to prosper.

Goal	Strategy
I. Integrate and promote quality management	Commit to a quality policy
	Market total quality and team building concepts
	Demonstrate management commitment
	Involve all levels
II. Build an organization responsive to customer needs and wants	Integrate quality into the business organization
	Educate the organization in quality concepts and methods
III. Consistently provide value to the customer	Build a foundation for improvement
	Apply quality techniques and tools for prevention
	Implement statistical quality control methods
IV. Achieve continuous improvement	Establish a quality education system
	Form audit systems
	Integrate total prevention
	Integrate total quality management

Figure 2   The Quality Master Plan

needs of the organization. The keys to continuous quality improvement that apply are:

Key #2: Total management commitment and support
Key #3: The building of trust and team spirit

The third goal is to *consistently provide value to the customer.* It defines the action plan, tools, and methods for the quality improvement process. The keys to continuous quality improvement that apply are:

Key #1: Continuous customer focus and satisfaction (both internal and external)
Key #4: Implementation of systems for prevention, measurement, and elimination of problems

If you think of the other goals as the brick and mortar and interior decoration of an office building, think of this goal as the powerhouse or energy that is needed to operate the building. Without a source of energy, the building will not be used and will fall into disrepair.

The fourth and final goal is to *achieve continuous improvement.* All the keys to quality apply to accomplish the fourth goal. Using the building analogy, the fourth goal is the system for maintaining, improving, and expanding the building structure and powerhouse (energy source). The fourth goal establishes an ongoing system for changing the way business is conducted.

Trust: The Achilles' Heel

Are people trustworthy? One of the principle ingredients of total management commitment and total quality in the organization is trust in the workplace. Building trust and team spirit is the third key to quality. Building trust is part of the quality master plan framework and should be integrated throughout the execution and implementation of the plan. Trust is a characteristic or an attribute of an individual or company and cannot be mandated by a decree from upper management. For most organizations, however, establishing and maintaining trust will greatly accelerate the level of achievement of the continuous quality improvement process. Trust cannot build quality into an organization, but achievement of quality can be enhanced by a foundation of trust.

The more mistrust in the organization the more difficult it will be to glean the type of information from employees that is needed to identify problems. The real expert in productivity improvement in any job is the person who holds that job. If an organization uses fear as part of its management style, employees are not likely to risk punishment and ridicule by pointing out problems and recommending solutions. The level of trust within an organization can be improved by group skills education (team building) and day-to-day management commitment. There is more to be gained by empowering people with responsibility and authority (i.e., trusting) than could ever be accomplished with a procedure or policy.

Example: At U-Trust Limited, a facility manager with a six-figure annual base salary plus bonuses, managing a half-billion-dollar-plus operation, does not have capital authority to purchase and install minor pieces of equipment.

In some cases, executives give managers responsibility but are not sure of the manager's ability to handle authority. A manager can be taught how to manage authority and can be given increasing amounts of authority over time. An organization should not paralyze itself with bureaucratic controls when the concern can be corrected with education. Employees who have distrust thrown in their faces often limit the scope of their responsibilities with a "not-my-job" mentality. *Building Trust in the Workplace* states, "When an organization is secretive, tightly controlled, does not delegate authority, and sharply separates management and management decisions from employees and lower level managers, it doesn't take much intelligence to recognize that management does not trust its 'underlings' to behave as reasonable, responsible people."*

A company executive of a Fortune 200 corporation felt that mistrust was the major roadblock to quality improvement. He stated, "Quality is when it is easier to sell internally than externally." Start your organization's commitment by cleaning out your warehouse of worn and ragged attitudes and replace them with attitudes that have greater utility. Make a paradigm shift in focus:

Out with . . .	In with . . .
• Quick-fix mentality.	• Taking action to prevent recurrence.
• "I told you so."	• "Let's do it right the first time."
• Shoot the messenger.	• Rewarding the pathfinder.
• Pointing the finger.	• "We're all in this together."
• Nine out of 10 times it's ok.	• 100 percent customer satisfaction.
• Them versus us.	• "We are a team."
• Corporate arrogance and fear.	• Self-confidence and humility.
• What the *hell* is going on?	• "Is there anything I can do to help?"
• It's close enough.	• Fitness for use . . .every time.

*Reprinted, by permission of publisher, from *AMA Review*, 2309, ©1984. American Management Association, New York. All rights reserved.

Trust can *not* stop at the personnel level. It must extend to the actions of managing the business. For example, an organization must have the self-discipline to ship only the products or provide only the services that the customer ordered.

Example: U-Trust Limited shipped substitute products without the customer's knowledge. This is intolerable for any reason. Knowing that constancy is an axiom of quality, and that variable raw materials will likely cause economic injury to its customer or the customer's customers, how can an organization justify or view unauthorized customer product substitution as anything but unscrupulous and unethical?

A business must take its lumps when inventory or production or resources are not properly managed. Honesty is the best policy and will always gain more customers in the long run. Furthermore, covering up the problem prevents action from being taken to prevent recurrence.

Benefits of the Quality Improvement Process

Many companies have demonstrated that quality pays, not by working harder or inspecting more, but by developing a new way of business and a new focus of doing things right the first time. To approach performance with an attitude of "we will do our best" or "strive for perfection, but allow for human error" is limiting and self-defeating. Such attitudes underlie the dramatic increase in U.S. customer demand for foreign-produced goods and services. In addition, many companies stand idly by while their U.S. counterparts take a competitive advantage by aggressively implementing the quality improvement process. Don't wait for the red ink, the time to act is now. Manage for success by building a strong, competitive, self-sufficient business environment.

> Don't wait for the red ink, the time to act is now.

The quality improvement process will benefit all facets of your business. A decision to invest in total quality management will give you one of the highest (if not *the* highest) discounted cash flows (DCFs) or return on investments (ROIs) of any project in your organization. Quality dollar benefits will come from:

- Cost savings.
- Productivity improvements (more proactive decisions and enhanced work environment).
- Elimination of waste.
- Increased sales.
- Reducing future uncertainty.

A conservative, documented accounting of a Fortune 500 company's quality savings included such factors as reductions in discounted off-grade sales, raw material wastes, inventories, and defective parts, along with improved yields and productivity. The survey revealed that in a six-year time span, the company received $10 in return for every $1 spent on quality education. The real number, once all the factors are considered, could be in the range of $20 return for every $1 spent on quality education. In another documented case, a quality control laboratory was able to reduce its overall analysis cost per unit produced by 20 percent over a short period.

The old assumption that the most economical way to operate is on the basis of allowed percent defects and errors is a myth. Operating on a basis of *doing it right the first time* is the most cost-effective. Additional savings will also come from areas harder to define, such as reduced insurance cost (stable operations), capital investment avoidance, increased output without adding personnel, and proactive versus defensive research and development.

In *Quality Without Tears* (page 5), Philip Crosby states that "production companies spend 20 percent or more of their sales dollars doing things wrong and doing them over. Service companies spend 35 percent or more of their operating costs doing things wrong and doing them over."

The quality process has aided, and in some cases has been the prime reason for the turnaround of typical GNP growth businesses into strategic, highly profitable concerns.

To summarize, the *do something* alternative that is the implementation of total quality management will benefit an organization in the following areas:

- Improved productivity.
- Elimination of waste.
- Increased profitability and competitiveness.
- Better work environment.

The *do nothing* alternative represents the advantage of lower risk to short-term profitability (a dubious plan) at the risk of the following:

- High risk of future loss of market shares (i.e., competitors implement the quality process).
- Moderate risk of increased appraisal costs (i.e., customers require evidence of quality improvement).

No matter how frequently you inspect, appraise, and double-check your products and services for quality, you will not be able to compete with businesses that have learned how to build quality into their products or services by *doing it right the first time.*

The name of the business game is survival of the fittest. To not merely survive, but to prosper, requires that business be able to meet fierce competition head on and also able to meet the challenges of a constantly changing environment. To ensure a prosperous future, every organization must balance its internal concerns with customer concerns while maintaining control over the cost of products and services. The future cannot be secured by technology, by new promotional campaigns, or just by working harder. Something different is needed to enable your organization to effect change. That "something" is a renewed focus on people and the implementation of the total quality improvement process. People and quality are the vital link to success in the 21st century.

SECTION II
GOALS AND
STRATEGIES

Objective: Change the organization culture (attitude) to a total quality way of management to improve competitiveness (survival) and to prosper.

Goal	Strategy
I. Integrate and promote quality management	Commit to a quality policy
	Market total quality and team building concepts
	Demonstrate management commitment
	Involve all levels
II. Build an organization responsive to customer needs and wants	Integrate quality into the business organization
	Educate the organization in quality concepts and methods
III. Consistently provide value to the customer	Build a foundation for improvement
	Apply quality techniques and tools for prevention
	Implement statistical quality control methods
IV. Achieve continuous improvement	Establish a quality education system
	Form audit systems
	Integrate total prevention
	Integrate total quality management

GOAL I: INTEGRATE AND PROMOTE QUALITY MANAGEMENT

This chapter and the next three chapters will provide you with the tools for implementing the goals of the quality master plan through a sequence of proven business strategies. As you read the four goal chapters, identify the elements that apply to your organization. Through this step-by-step program, you will work toward the overall objective of the quality master plan which is to *change the organization culture (attitude) to a total quality way of management to improve competitiveness and to prosper.*

The achievement of Goal I, *integrate and promote quality management,* may be outlined in terms of four major strategies, each of which in turn requires several steps (Figure 3). These strategies are to:

- Commit to a quality policy.
- Market total quality and team-building concepts.
- Demonstrate management commitment.
- Involve all levels.

Commit to a Quality Policy

The first important strategy is to achieve and demonstrate management commitment to quality as a concept and as a goal. The steps to achieving the strategies to Goal I are to:

1. Evaluate policies of other companies.
2. Define requirements for a quality policy.
3. Draft and circulate a quality policy. (Solicit organizational inputs and contributions which will help develop ownership of the quality policy.)
4. Publish the quality policy to demonstrate to all employees that upper management is committed to the process (a *quality milestone*).

27

Commit to a quality policy

Evaluate policies
Define policy requirements
Draft policy and circulate for comments
Publish policy

Market total quality and team-building concepts

Plan promotion campaign events
Select media

Demonstrate management commitment

Complete education
Take a leadership role in the quality team
Advocate quality and support champions

Involve all levels

Define criteria for involvement
Conduct periodic assessment

(Also refer to plan schedule in *Section III — Help*)

Figure 3   Goal I Detail Chart

Publication of a formal quality policy is your first quality milestone. This policy statement should be brief and understandable by every employee. It should contain these elements:

- The quality standard.
- A customer focus.
- Provision for continuous improvement.

Although most companies kick off their quality process with a quality process mission statement, some organizations develop separate mission statements for the customers, employees, the corporation, and the community. Your quality policy can be derived from the quality triad components (requirements, expectations, and value). For example: The (your company name) Company will consistently provide products and services that meet our customers' requirements and have value.

The quality schedule plan (see *Section III — Help*) shows that the company quality policy should be developed early in the implementation process. The management commitment to a quality policy provides a central focus for all employees and demonstrates that you mean business.

Market the Concepts of Total Quality and Team Building

Both total quality and team building must be promoted within the organization as well as in the marketplace. The steps in this strategy include the following:

1. Identifying promotional opportunities:
   a. Quality policy
   b. Success stories
   c. Achievement of milestones
   d. Individual recognition
   e. Quality events and similar activities

2. Selecting promotional media (announcements, booklets, videotapes, bulletin boards) and the message focus (directive, customer orientation, educational).

Promotion is essential for keeping everyone focused on the importance of quality to the organization. Promotion alone will not change attitudes or behaviors that have been established for years, but it is a reminder of management's commitment. Promotion of a new car in the newspapers will not sell the car, but it may convince potential customers to go to the showroom and take a look at the new model.

Every promotional campaign must relate to some management action or achievement. A superficial effort will be detected immediately. In corporations across the United States, employees have seen many programs come and go (student body left . . . then student body right). Throughout these cycles, employees (exempt and nonexempt) have absorbed certain principles that are detrimental to the quality effort, such as:

"Volume is always more important than quality.
(All the junk gets sold anyway!)"

"Team players tend to get passed over and are easy targets
when things are not going well."

"The bigger the better."

"No investment in quality was ever justified."

You should expect to commit to a high level of promotional activity (see the schedule plan in *Section III — Help*) during the initial phases of the quality implementation plan. First you will need to decide how your quality message should be transmitted. Executives and managers can do any of the following: (1) make personal presentations to all employees, (2) prepare slide presentations and videotapes for employees to view on their own, (3) issue written directives, and (4) any combination of these. You will need an ongoing promotion maintenance program after the initial phases are completed. The marketing campaign can be handled internally or sub-contracted to advertising campaign experts.

Demonstrate Management Commitment

A convincing demonstration of management commitment is needed to counter skepticism, fear, and inertia. The steps in this strategy consist of the following:

1. Completing all quality education.
2. Taking a leadership role in a quality team.
3. Advocating quality and supporting champions.

Quality management strategy will not be achieved unless management takes an active role in its execution and implementation. Initially, managers should expect to devote approximately 10 to 25 percent of their time to supporting the quality improvement process. When managers are first exposed to the quality process implementation requirements, many indicate they don't have time for quality. Paradoxically, analysis of a typical manager's day would reveal that his or her time is consumed by handling recurring problems, doing things over, and managing defects and errors. *In every case where quality management has been successfully implemented, valuable management time has been saved.* A successful quality program tends to give managers more time to be proactive in business initiatives rather than reacting to constant problems (i.e., putting out fires). Given the overwhelming evidence thus far, can you afford not to commit the time necessary to implement a quality management system?

Management's commitment should take the form of supporting the process through dedication to quality concepts (see *The Quality Master Plan: An Overview,* page 13). This is accomplished by focusing on the process, not on specific volume or price goals. Opportunities to show commitment include attendance at quality education sessions and leadership of quality teams. Dedication to quality concepts can be accomplished by written or oral statements (public and internal) that show personal and organizational commitment.

> . . . recognition of team achievements and individual performance.

The last, but perhaps the most important aspect of management commitment, is recognition of team achievements and individual performance. Teams and individuals should receive public and private praise for achieving milestones in the implementation of the quality process. If the quality effort is not focused at the individual level, the organization will be sending mixed signals to employees. Every individual's performance rating must reflect the new, quality way of doing business. Recognition should be given to the number of *quality units*, *quality services*, and *quality new products*, not to the number or volume of units, services, and new products.

Example: Paul received a high performance rating for introducing a new product in record time. Rachel, who focused her resources on prevention (by defining the quality triad components and a system to meet those requirements), received very little recognition because her product introduction took 20 percent longer than Paul's. A closer look revealed that only 30 percent of Paul's product was marketable and the rest had to be sent back for redesign, while Rachel's product was designed right the first time. Over the year, Rachel's product cost less to develop (no rework) and resulted in more profit to the business. Clearly, Rachel should be rewarded for her prevention style of management and contribution to the company.

Management decisions and actions must be:

- Objective.
- Uniformly applied.
- Job related.

Example: An executive of a Fortune 500 corporation conducted a grueling, all-day individual review of an organization's volume performance compared to goals but failed to include any reference to quality in the review. Later that evening at a quality recognition dinner, the executive gave a talk on improving the system for a prevention style of management. How consistent were these actions with the quality process the manager was expressing? Talk is cheap!

Management commitment to the quality improvement process is never-ending. Continuous management commitment supports employees who have adopted the new way of doing business and is an outward demonstration that management is serious.

Involve All Levels of Your Organization

The following two major strategies are required to involve all levels of the organization in the quality effort:

1. Define criteria for involvement in the organization quality plan.
2. Conduct periodic assessment (measurement) of employee involvement.

All employees must be educated in the quality concepts and involved in the quality process implementation to some degree. Quality is not the responsibility of any single individual (i.e., the quality control manager). It is everyone's responsibility, in every facet of the business. Minimum requirements may be set for participation in the process implementation phases so that everyone understands the quality expectations. Once quality management is implemented, there will be total involvement since the organization has changed its way of doing business.

GOAL II: BUILD AN ORGANIZATION RESPONSIVE TO CUSTOMER NEEDS AND WANTS

To be responsive to customers, your organization must provide an appropriate business infrastructure. The quality organization is the forum for channeling quality issues and concerns and ensuring that they are given the proper priority.

Quality education gives everyone the same foundation of quality principles, the same vocabulary for effective communication, and the same history which allows for bonding in the corporation. Like a driver's license certifying an individual's knowledge of rules, strategies, and regulations which prevent chaos on the highways, quality education provides the assurance that everyone is starting from the same knowledge base.

The achievement of Goal II, *build an organization responsive to customer needs and wants*, is outlined in terms of two major strategies, each of which requires several steps (Figure 4). These strategies are to:

- Integrate quality into the business organization.
- Educate the organization in quality concepts and methods.

Integrate Quality into the Business Organization

To build an organization that responds promptly and flexibly to the needs and wants of its customers requires that the quality process be fully integrated into all aspects of business operations. The objective is not simply to establish another program but to *change the way your business is conducted by making quality management part of that business.* Creating a separate organization to enforce quality standards may be in direct conflict with the goal of integration. In some ways a small business may have a great advan-

33

Objective: Change the organization culture (attitude) to a total quality way of management to improve competitiveness (survival) and to prosper.

Goal	Strategy
I. Integrate and promote quality management	*Commit to a quality policy*
	Market total quality and team building concepts
	Demonstrate management commitment
	Involve all levels
II. Build an organization responsive to customer needs and wants	*Integrate quality into the business organization*
	Educate the organization in quality concepts and methods
III. Consistently provide value to the customer	*Build a foundation for improvement*
	Apply quality techniques and tools for prevention
	Implement statistical quality control methods
IV. Achieve continuous improvement	*Establish a quality education system*
	Form audit systems
	Integrate total prevention
	Integrate total quality management

Integrate quality into the business organization

Appoint a quality coordinator or director
Establish a quality management team
Form quality business team
Organize quality action teams

Educate the organization in quality concepts and methods

Plan and develop education strategies
Quality management seminar
Quality awareness education
Quality action skills education
Quality process implementation education

(Also refer to plan schedule in *Section III — Help*)

Figure 4   Goal II Detail Chart

tage over a large corporation merely because it can readily integrate quality management into the existing structure.

In a large corporation, however, it may be necessary to define a separate sub-structure for the initial quality effort to ensure that it receives the proper priority and can be monitored. There is no single right answer, but to achieve the long-term goal quality management must be integrated (ingrained) into the way the business is operated. Specific strategies for achieving integration must be tailored to meet your individual organization's needs based on environment, culture, and nature of the business.

The steps presented here are typical of an organizational structure that many companies have used in their quality improvement process. To minimize confusion, the team and committee titles used in the steps to integrate quality are commonly used throughout industry. For example, Quality Management Committee is similar to Management Committee or Operating Committee, and the Quality Business Team is similar to Business Team. The Quality Action Team could be formed from first-line management teams already in existence.

The following steps (Figure 4) are proposed:

1. Appoint a director or coordinator of quality.
2. Establish a Quality Management Committee.
3. Form quality business teams.
4. Organize and develop quality action teams (quality milestone).

Whatever organizational structure is decided upon, it needs to be well thought out to meet present and anticipated organizational needs. Many organizational structures are available to you and several factors that you should consider in forming your quality organization are outlined in the following sections. The formation of teams is a good way to get everyone involved in the process, but you should make sure they are not stymied with bureaucracy and politics. The top of the organization should consist of a cross-functional team to focus on external customer awareness, and to provide resources and direction. At lower levels, however, cross-functional teams may not be effective because team members may be unable to put aside their hidden agendas, turf issues, and egos. If they cannot do so, they will not be effective in finding root-cause solutions (problem solving). Cross-functional team effectiveness can be improved by using facilitators and by providing group leaders with group training skills that will enable them to address motivation and team building head on.

> The formation of teams is a good way to get everyone involved . . .

Quality action teams are the nucleus of the successful quality improvement program. They should be line-oriented (i.e., marketing, manufacturing, distribution, etc.) to develop team spirit in solving problems and achieving quality goals. Given the proper support, the progress of some of the action teams can be phenomenal. The upper level teams need to continually assess whether they are helping or hindering the action teams' progress. If the quality action team is running smoothly, upper management should allow it autonomy. The upper level teams must focus on removing barriers to continuous quality improvement.

Appoint a Quality Coordinator (Director)

The quality director is responsible for ensuring that the procedures and policies support quality products and services throughout all business functions of the organization. Ideally, the quality director and the head of the company should be the same person. Creating a new position tends to make quality a separate department or program and adds a layer of management. The quality process should transcend all departments and functions. Many quality "gurus" strongly recommend that for large organizations a new director or vice president of quality be appointed to show that management is committed to quality and that quality has a high priority. The top quality administrator (director) should be a full-fledged member of the decision-making team of the company (management committee, operations committee, etc.). Note that the quality director is *not* another name for the quality control or quality assurance manager. The quality director is part of the leadership team for the company's quality management effort. The team leaders include every executive, every manager, every supervisor, and every section or group leader.

Establish a Quality Management Team

In a total quality management organization (Figure 5), the quality management team (steering committee or quality improvement council) forms the cross-functional team that leads the quality improvement process. Members of the team include the top quality administrator along, with top level management. The team is responsible for planning, monitoring, providing resources, and setting priorities for the implementation of the quality improvement process. Participation cannot be delegated.

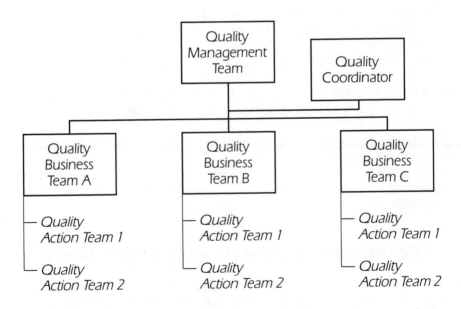

Figure 5   The Total Quality Organization

Form Quality Business Teams

The quality business team identifies internal and external customer requirements and expectations. It provides direction, sets priorities (see action item list, page 106), defines, and monitors the quality action plan to ensure that problems and defects do not recur.

The quality business teams should focus on the management of a business or operating unit. Alternative names for the function include quality boards, quality improvement teams, and site teams. Characteristically, the quality board or quality business team members should:

- Represent the various functions supporting the business or site.
- Have the authority to commit resources.
- Be well-balanced in levels of authority. (This may depend on company culture.)
- Include one quality assurance representative.
- Select a chairperson (*not* the quality assurance representative).

A typical *product* quality business team should be composed of the following:

- Manufacturing — plant manager or superintendent.
- Technology — process engineering or research and development manager.
- Commercial — business manager or marketing manager.
- Quality — quality assurance manager.
- Other members (organizationally dependent) — purchasing, distribution, sales, technical service, and customer service.

A *service* quality business team should include the service manager and operations manager.

The composition of your quality business team for product- or service-related businesses will depend on the leadership functions in your organization.

Organize and Develop Quality Action Teams

The foundation of the quality organization structure is the quality action team. The unit or department quality action team will use quality improvement tools and problem-solving techniques to provide products or services that consistently meet customer needs and expectations (quality triad components). These teams are formed along natural leadership and line functions (i.e., natural work groups) within an organization. These are people who are close enough to the process to identify problems and root-cause solutions. The action team can be composed of managers, supervisors, specialists, and exempt, nonexempt, hourly, and salary employees. Special action teams may be formed to address specific problem areas. Each quality action team is responsible for its portion of the quality action plan and action item list. As a general rule, the leadership of special action teams should be taken by the person or department representative who has ownership of the problem (i.e., where the problem exists).

The action item list is a collection of issues, problems, or concerns that must be resolved for continuous quality improvement. The items may come from either the quality business team or the quality action teams. The list should include the following:

- A description of the action item.
- The benefits of correcting the defect and taking action to prevent recurrence.
- The individual and function responsible for resolution (i.e., operations, service, sales, production, technology, marketing).
- A target date for completion.

More information on the action item list appears in *5. Goal III: Consistently Provide Value to the Customer* and *Section III — Help.*

The quality schedule plan (see *Section III — Help*) indicates the steps and possible timing for the quality team formation. The quality business and action teams are responsible for taking action to prevent recurrence, and their activation represents a milestone in the quality improvement process.

In summary, the quality organization structure should be flexible and compatible with the business environment. What is important is that the organization developed is responsive to customer expectations and needs.

Educate the Organization in Quality Concepts and Methods

Educating the organization in quality concepts and methods is essential to the success of the quality improvement process. If individuals don't know the rules of the road, there will be utter chaos and confusion. Quality education provides the framework and mind set for *doing it right the first time.* The following is a list of the steps involved in this strategy:

1. Planning and development of groups and determining the education strategies.
2. Pre-education evaluation and an action plan.
3. Quality management seminar for upper level management.
4. Quality awareness education for all employees (quality milestone).

5. Group action skills education for team leaders.
6. Quality process implementation education for special tools and quality techniques for overcoming roadblocks and ensuring that the quality plan succeeds.

Education in quality principles and concepts is required for successful implementation of the quality improvement process, just as education is required for the successful start-up of a new business, plant, or process. This is part of doing it right the first time compared to making time to do it right the second time.

The priorities of the quality education process should be:

1. Education in the need for quality and the associated quality concepts.
2. Quality training in the tools and methods of the quality process.
3. Group action skills education for management leadership and direction.

A basic premise of the education program is that quality is an organizational function, that is, quality is the responsibility of each member of an organization. The focus on people and their responsibility is crucial to the success of the quality process (i.e., to the future success of the business). Each course or seminar should be created with that focus in mind.

Planning and Development of Education Strategies

Thorough planning must precede actual education efforts. First, what are the educational requirements of your organization? Quality awareness? Group skills? Statistical quality control? Cost of quality? The setting and format should be evaluated. These may consist of lectures, workshops, formal classes, forums, videotapes, computer simulations, correspondence courses, or any combination of these.

Internal and external resources should be reviewed and their utilization planned. Options for cross-functional groups may be evaluated as compared with natural-line groups such as work groups. Learning objectives and optimal group sizes should be defined.

Pre-Education Evaluation and Action Plan

The formation of the classes and the quality action teams should be well planned. Ideally, the education groups and the quality action teams would be the same composition. However, for a variety of reasons (i.e., number of locations, business organization, job requirements, size of the company, etc.)

this may not be possible. In some cases, cross-functional groups may satisfy some special education or team-building requirement of the organization. Assign one person the responsibility of coordinating the education program. Determine specific goals and relative time frames (see Help section, quality plan schedule). Analyze the organization and define quality education groups.

Define participants' responsibilities and conduct an assessment of their skills and backgrounds. Determine the logistical requirements for both the recordkeeping and training areas of each educational unit. Hold a supervisor planning meeting to discuss expectations and implementation of the quality education. Establish a quality structure or organization for immediate follow-up of quality education.

Quality Management Seminars

The quality management seminars should be designed to introduce company executives and managers to the quality process. Managers and executives need to understand how quality will impact their organization and their role in the implementation process. To manage quality you must understand quality. In small business organizations the quality management seminar can be combined with the quality awareness course.

Quality Awareness Education

Quality awareness education is a forum for understanding the following: (1) quality concepts and purpose; (2) the definition of quality; (3) tools for quality process implementation (i.e., problem solving, customer/supplier requirements, statistical quality control); and (4) the business quality structure and team expectations. The duration and course emphasis should be varied depending on the education target group's objectives and needs. If the quality awareness education is followed up with immediate commitment and support, the organization will be well on its way to overcoming a major hurdle to process implementation (i.e., ownership of the new process).

> To manage quality you must understand quality.

Group Action Skills Education

Group action skills education has significant added value for expediting the execution of the quality improvement process. Many companies have indicated that the company culture is often the major roadblock to the successful implementation of the quality process. A 1987 survey conducted by The Gallup Organization for ASQC revealed that 43 percent of 615 top-level executives regarded a change in corporate culture — including management initiative — as integral to achieving quality improvement (a three-fold increase over the 1986 survey). Group action skills education will develop team leaders who are able to handle the changes occurring in the organization to ensure the success of the quality process transition. The education will provide tools for coping with mixed signals from the top as well as resistance to change from the bottom (breaking down "Us versus Them" barriers). The scope and extent of group skills education will depend on the assessment of organizational needs.

Stress consultants claim that people develop skills to survive in their current environment, and that during times of stress they revert to the familiar. Group action skills will provide leaders with the tools to keep everyone moving toward quality improvement. In many cases the change from old corporate values to new quality values will create stress and insecurity.

Example: For Paul's entire corporate life, he was told that pounds or units of output are more important than quality. The rule was to "never stop producing." Now, he is told that those rules were all wrong and new rules are that "no pound or unit should be produced unless it is a quality product. If it is not a quality pound or unit, press the stop button." Paul is forced to change his entire way of thinking and doing his work. Without quality education and management support, Paul will be reluctant to choose quality over "putting out the pounds" during times of high stress.

The group action skills education should be designed to meet your individual organizational culture. A decision to train team leaders in group action skills will only help the speedy implementation of the quality process; a decision not to provide group action skills education could result in a significant quality process roadblock.

Quality Process Implementation Education

Quality process implementation education for team leaders is the critical support and follow-up step needed for implementation of the quality process. Too often an organization focuses solely on the quality awareness training and later asks itself, "Why isn't something happening? We trained everyone!" What is missing is quality tools development, follow-up, and implementation of the quality process after quality education. Management should support implementation by:

1. Developing a quality action team mission and objective.
2. Monitoring the progress of the quality improvement process.
3. Providing special skills training to support individual and team requirements.

42

Bridging the classroom education and application for a specific job function will make or break the success of the quality improvement process.

The follow-up education phase is supported by: internal quality professionals, facilitators, outside consultants, training specialists, and quality engineering resources. The follow-up vehicles are written documentation (guidelines), a quality hotline, conference style forums, formal classrooom education, and one-on-one contact meetings. Take the above ingredients (resources and vehicles) and apply them to the organizational quality process requirements.

The team mission statement and the quality implementation objectives can be supported by written guidelines and reinforced by conference style meetings of the team leaders. Informal one-on-one contact meetings may be needed to support individual team leaders that have a total mental block on how the quality improvement process relates to their daily department, business, or individual performance.

Example: Twelve months had elapsed after quality awareness education had taken place and a department manager had not taken the first step to implement the quality improvement process. The corporate staff department manager could not visualize how quality applied to his group. A one-on-one conference with the department manager involved applying brainstorming techniques which opened the door for action. Before the meeting, the manager made statements like, "We work hard. I have good people who do a professional job. We are understaffed. It takes time to put together the assessments." After the meetings, he made the quality observations that:

- The customers were pleased with the quality of the output but were unhappy about the response time.
- Fifty percent of the professionals' work was repetitive and could be put on a computer or turned over to a clerk or secretary.
- The filing system and records maintenance was a mess and the professionals lost valuable time trying to keep current and routing out needed documents.
- The staff offices looked like poorly maintained warehouses because there was inadequate storage space for documents and information.
- Valuable time was lost training new secretaries because of the high turnover due to the chaotic filing systems and lack of office organization.

Example: In another case a corrective action team (a team formed to solve problems) spent nine months trying to define the term *corrective action team*. Somehow the team became caught up in terminology, rather than applying its skills to solving problems. A good support system could have avoided the loss in resources.

Example: Manufacturing put together a $1 million capital investment proposal partially based on quality savings. The investment would significantly improve the product quality and control competitive product differences. The proposal did not receive business management or accounting department support because they did not understand the concepts of the cost of quality. The result was that marketing and sales continued to struggle in the marketplace and blamed manufacturing for not fixing the product. At the same time, manufacturing received a strong message that quality improvement is nice to talk about, but don't take it seriously. After several failures to acquire capital resources to solve root causes, the management quality education weakness was identified and corrected. However, it was at a significant cost of profits and negative attitudes toward the quality improvement process.

The matrix for sustaining the quality awareness education is shown in Figure 6.

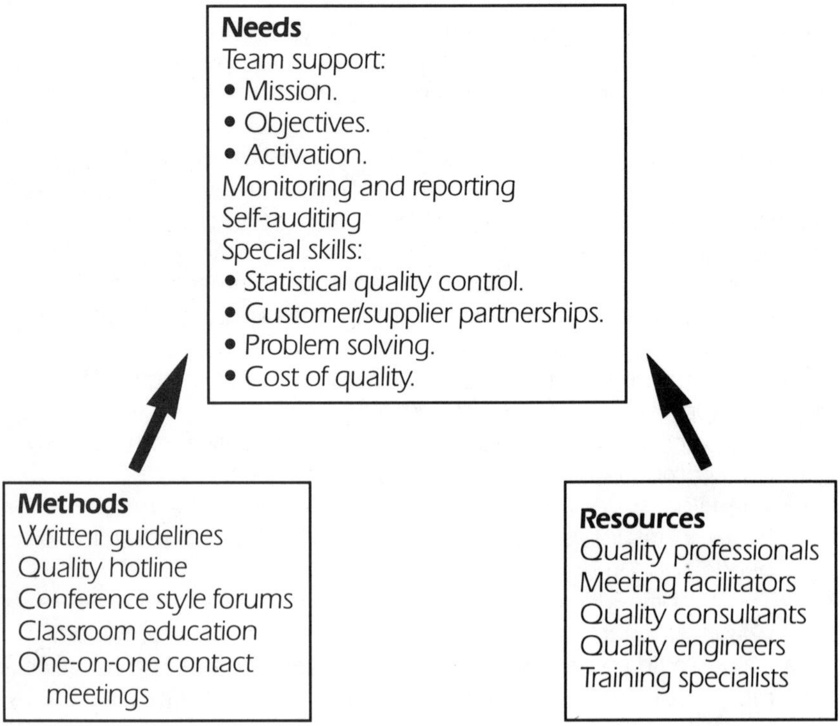

Needs
Team support:
• Mission.
• Objectives.
• Activation.
Monitoring and reporting
Self-auditing
Special skills:
• Statistical quality control.
• Customer/supplier partnerships.
• Problem solving.
• Cost of quality.

Methods
Written guidelines
Quality hotline
Conference style forums
Classroom education
One-on-one contact
   meetings

Resources
Quality professionals
Meeting facilitators
Quality consultants
Quality engineers
Training specialists

Figure 6   Quality Education Matrix — Follow-Up Phase

GOAL III: CONSISTENTLY PROVIDE VALUE TO THE CUSTOMER

To consistently provide value, the organization must have the management systems for gathering data, maintaining uniformity, and preventing defects and errors. To provide the maximum value, the supplier organization must be able to *do it right the first time.* The foundation for improvement and problem prevention systems is learning how to do it right.

Consistency and uniformity provide the core for many quality improvement processes that have variable outputs. Many processes and systems are either under or over controlled which results in wide-range, inconsistent outputs. Statistical quality control methods reduce variability, identify out of control points, and provide a uniform method of control. Three strategies are needed (Figure 7) to consistently provide value to the customer. The completion of each strategy requires several steps.

The strategies for accomplishing Goal III include the following:

- Build a foundation for improvement.
- Apply quality techniques and tools for problem prevention: the problem, measurement, solution, action (PMSA) system.
- Implement statistical quality control methods.

Build a Foundation for Improvement

Building a foundation for improvement requires an understanding and application of steps for management action and data/information-gathering systems.

The steps for building a foundation for improvement are:

1. Initiate the process and immediately start to list known customer complaints, known product or service problems, and known opportunities for improvement (quality milestone).

45

Objective: Change the organization culture (attitude) to a total quality way of management to improve competitiveness (survival) and to prosper.

Goal	Strategy
I. Integrate and promote quality management	Commit to a quality policy
	Market total quality and team building concepts
	Demonstrate management commitment
	Involve all levels
II. Build an organization responsive to customer needs and wants	Integrate quality into the business organization
	Educate the organization in quality concepts and methods
III. Consistently provide value to the customer	Build a foundation for improvement
	Apply quality techniques and tools for prevention
	Implement statistical quality control methods
IV. Achieve continuous improvement	Establish a quality education system
	Form audit systems
	Integrate total prevention
	Integrate total quality management

Build a foundation for improvement

Initialize the process
Develop an action item list
Publish a quality action plan
Identify customers/suppliers and their requirements
Develop a supply/demand outreach program
Customer CPR

Apply quality techniques and prevention tools

Apply PMSA system to problem solving

Implement statistical quality control methods

Select a SQC method
Implement SQC pilot process
Expand SQC to remaining operations
Bring process in control and make capable
Qualify suppliers

(Also refer to plan schedule in *Section III — Help*)

Figure 7   Goal III Detail Chart

2. Develop an action item list (itemize the issue, responsibility, benefits, and target date for completion) and publish as part of quality action plan.
3. Publish a quality action plan (quality milestone).
4. Identify customers/suppliers and their agreed upon requirements and expectations.
5. Develop a supply/demand outreach program.
6. Establish a customer CPR (complaint/problems/response) program for collecting and responding to customer complaints and ideas for improvement (quality milestone).

The quality schedule plan (see *Section III — Help*) shows that many of these strategy steps can be started before everyone is trained. A quicker transition from classroom training to hands-on implementation will significantly increase the value and effectiveness of the training. A frequent criticism of many training programs is that there is no organizational follow-up and support after the training and education.

Initiate the Process

The quality action teams and business teams can start immediately by brainstorming known quality issues in your department or business. Ask yourself whether you have consistently provided products/services that have value and utility (quality triad) to the receiver. The problems may be related to the actual product or service, or they may reflect internal hassles that prevent the job from being *done right the first time.* Now is the time to encourage everyone to list all those gripes and complaints that have been *preventing them from doing their job right or causing them to keep solving Problem #27 over and over again.*

At first people may be somewhat reluctant to expose problems for fear of reprisal (we always shoot the bearer of bad news). Leaders need to ensure they are in a position to defend everyone's right to speak up and to keep the discussion focused on the business objectives (making a quality product or service) and away from personalities.

Example: What would you do in this situation? You hold a team meeting to ask if there are any problems with the Sprocket production line. There is silence in the room. Finally, your lieutenant says that there must not be any problems, and that the Sprocket line is running like a well-oiled machine. You don't accept the silence as an endorsement that there are no problems, so you press harder to get information. Finally, the silence is broken when Paul speaks up by stating that no one has listened before or that there are so many problems that it is useless even to try to list them all. Paul has never encountered someone (supervisor or manager) who is actually going to *listen and take action* on his concerns.

Before labeling Paul a troublemaker who has a poor attitude, consider all the other employees who haven't offered to share any real information. You must be open to all opportunities to encourage team participation in the problem-solving process.

Nonparticipation and fear are problems at all management levels . . .

First, the leader should congratulate Paul for his willingness to speak up. Then use this opportunity to explain why this program is different and try to sell the benefits of the quality process. Restate that you and the team are there to listen and to consider all the issues and complaints. Paul's speaking up is a test of sincerity and trust and was what everyone was thinking but afraid to say. It would be much easier for Paul to keep his mouth shut. If no one like Paul existed in the organization and everyone repeated the standard dogma, there could be a serious roadblock to improving quality. If the situation is handled properly, Paul will probably become the strongest supporter of the quality improvement process and be a leader in the sub-culture.

Nonparticipation and fear are problems at all management levels, and in fact, the problem becomes worse in the higher levels of management right on up to the board room. "Silence is golden" has long been the key for job security and advancement. The result has been mediocrity and lack of business renewal. The point is that *the leader must empower people to participate in the process* (apply group action skills) to get the best possible input.

A group action technique for soliciting input from team members in a safe, nonthreatening environment is "brainstorming." Brainstorming is a form of creative thinking in which ideas about a particular topic are solicited in a nonjudgmental, unrestricted manner from all members of a group. It is an effective technique to elicit perceived problems for the business, unit, or department. Obtaining input (problems, concerns, and issues) is the first step in getting problems out in the open so that they can be resolved once and for all.

The need for formal training group action skills depends on the business environment and the individual manager's group process skills. If the work environment is stressful, competitive, and threatening, group dynamic skills are critical to the overall success of the quality improvement process.

Develop an Action Item List

The action item list is your scorecard. It shows progress in the quality improvement process and evaluates the impact of the quality teams. Complex operational problems may require special action teams (task forces, corrective action teams, etc.).

List and categorize the issues by subject, assigning responsibility for each item; estimate benefits and target dates for completion of each item. Don't confine your focus to the most difficult issue to the exclusion of all other concerns. Individuals must be held accountable for the action items to ensure that the problem is given the proper priority. A list of benefits for solving the problem will motivate your organization to correct and prevent defects. The cost of quality (COQ) should be used to show benefits as potential dollar savings to the business. The COQ savings are derived from the elimination of rechecking and reworking (inspection and correction of errors). Organizations like individuals take action when there is justification. The benefits for solving a package identification problem are shown in *PMSA Root-Cause Solutions, Exhibit E*, page 109.

Initially, many of the inputs of the action teams may center on quality of work life issues. Usually, when individuals are exposed to the quality process, their first thoughts reflect internal hassles and issues which prevent them from doing their job right the first time. Many of these work life issues are self-imposed but others are a direct result of management systems. Whether perceived or real, each issue should be treated objectively and thoroughly. For quality's sake, don't sweep them under the rug! Some typical work life issues include the following:

- Operators are required to take samples to the control laboratory causing the process to be left unattended.
- Malfunctioning vehicles cause delays of deliveries.
- Lack of information sharing causes poor decision making.
- Shortage of parts, tools, and equipment causes delays in correcting problems.
- Lack of training for special skill job requirements causes poor performance.

A few of the issues on your action item list will have obvious root-cause solutions and can be corrected quickly. However, most of the issues will be more complicated and will require a data-gathering step (see *Apply the PMSA System to Problem Solvings*, page 56-62).

Publish your initial action item list as part of the quality action plan and update it monthly or at each quality team meeting. Turn to *Section III — Help* to review the sample action item lists for manufacturing, materials management, service management, and marketing (also see *PMSA Root-Cause Solutions, Exhibit A*, page 106).

Publish a Quality Action Plan

Your quality action plan can be as simple as stating the purpose (mission) and goals for a specified time period (e.g., one year). You can also make a more elaborate plan by the addition of procedures and guidelines for the quality initiative for every department, division, or business. The action plan contents could include the following:

- Your quality policy.
- The objective and scope of the program.
- Key opportunities for the coming year.
- Organization and responsibilities.
- Quality action plans for functional areas:
  - Materials management.
  - Operations.
  - Transportation and distribution.
  - Sales and marketing.
  - Technology.
  - Quality assurance.
- Audits.
- Employee recognition program.
- Data management systems (computer- and procedural-based).

The American National Standard ANSI/ASQC Q94-1987 (published by ASQC) and the Malcolm Baldrige National Quality Award criteria suggest that a quality plan and a quality manual are needed to implement a quality improvement process. The quality action plan (or business quality plan) described previously provides the business direction, quality policy, business objectives, and defines the organizational structure. The quality manual is a collection of specific standards and procedures that must be followed to ensure uniform, consistent, and reliable outputs from the organization or institution.

Identify Customers/Suppliers and Their Requirements

Define the customers and suppliers affecting your department or business. Every process has inputs and outputs and every activity performed has a customer and a supplier. The process can involve making a product for an external customer or receiving a service from an internal supplier (individual, coworker, or supervisor). An example of an internal customer is a subordinate turning in a monthly report to his or her manager or reporting sales data to the accounting department. Meeting internal customer needs and expectations becomes the very foundation for everyone's job. Defining who the customers are and what they need will open doors for *doing it right the first time* every time, for every process.

Example: BA Team Industries was concerned because its product had more "zip" than the competing products. Management initiated a long-term research project to reduce the level of "zip" comparable to that of its competitors. Meanwhile, a customer survey revealed that BA Team Industries' largest market *liked* the high level of "zip." Unfortunately, BA Team Industries chose to disregard the customer's input (what do customers know about the product anyway?). BA Team Industries focused all of its attention and concern on the competitive product specifications and analysis. The customers' requirements, expectations, and values were not taken seriously. BA Team Industries spent another 18 months on research then announced a price increase to counteract eroding product margins. A loss in market share had been forecast due to anticipated customers switching to other suppliers. What happened instead was that customers didn't switch suppliers because the added "zip" was a tangible benefit! When customers used the BA Team Industries' product, their equipment operated more smoothly and there was 20 percent less down time for contamination and fouling clean up.

Before this turn of events, BA Team Industries did not take its customers' needs and expectations into account. Afterward, defensive research was eliminated in favor of developing new products for entry into new markets and capitalizing on the added self-cleaning features of its product with the added "zip." It was the competition, then, who had to spend research dollars to develop a product with the added "zip" the customers were now expecting.

The important point is that managers and action teams must be aware of who their customers/suppliers are and what they expect.

> Build on success by completing each step and moving closer to continuous quality improvement.

Develop a Supply/Demand Outreach Program

A good starting point is the establishment of a good customer/supplier outreach program. You can start with a project (task) approach. Use flow charts, process evaluation summaries, and requirement worksheets to help organize your project (process) in terms of inputs/outputs and requirements. Build on success by completing each step and moving closer to continuous quality improvement. Separate programs are needed for the demand and supply side for both internal and external customers.

Typically, a customer/supplier is thought of as the one who purchases the product or supplies the service external to the organization. This idea needs to be expanded to include all the internal customers and suppliers to the organization. Each person, department, and function receives inputs and provides outputs, so all are customers and suppliers. If internal customer/supplier requirements and expectations are met, then a major step has been taken to satisfy the external customers/suppliers of the finished product or service.

Demand Side (Internal and External Customers). The basic steps for the demand side of a customer-oriented outreach program consist of the following:

1. Self-assessment.
2. Field verification.
3. Ongoing analysis of feedback.

You can start by conducting a self-assessment of customer (internal and external) requirements and expectations. First, define all of your products and services. Next, identify the actual customers. (Who benefits from the work? Who depends on your output?) Finally, define the customers' needs and wants and identify the quality triad components.

The second step, the field verification, calls for you to meet the customer and complete the field verification requirements. The field verification requirements must be well thought out and planned to ensure that there is mutual agreement of requirements and that a positive relationship is maintained.

To accomplish the third step, you should continue to seek customer feedback for continuous, never-ending improvement. Handling customer feedback (complaints, dislikes, recommendations, criticism) can be an especially sensitive topic. If handled properly, the payback is the development of trust, mutual respect, and a satisfied customer.

Supply Side (Vendor and Internal Suppliers). The basic steps for the supply side of a customer-oriented outreach program consist of the following:

1. Self-assessment.
2. Supplier quality awareness meeting (group).
3. Supplier meeting (one-on-one).

The outputs of any process are directly affected by its inputs. To receive consistent and uniform inputs, you need to develop a supplier/customer partnership. The partnership may require exchange of information and evaluation of quality assurance activities and procedures.

First, conduct a self-assessment of your requirements and identify potential suppliers (both internal and external). Identify primary and secondary suppliers.

The second step is to share your quality improvement focus by conducting a supplier quality awareness meeting. The meeting should be used to define your quality objectives, obtain supplier quality commitment, and serve as a vehicle for developing awareness of the quality improvement process.

Third, meet with your suppliers (one-on-one) to establish clear, mutually understood requirements. Get the supplier's reaction to the requirements and evaluate other wants that could have added value.

53

Note: The supplier's qualification section later in this chapter deals with the qualitative aspects of a supplier's (product or service) quality process and acceptability.

Customer surveys can provide insight into the customer's perception and use of your organization's product or service. Some service industries center their entire marketing program around getting customer feedback in focus team meetings. The key to gaining customer/supplier partnerships is to listen to the customers' wants and needs and then to supply the appropriate product or service for everyone's benefit.

Establish a Customer CPR (Complaint/Problem/Response) Program

You will need a formal system to record, investigate, and respond to the complaints of customers. Complaints can be divided into three classifications: product or service, distribution, and documentation errors (see *Section III — Help, Customer, CPR Complaint Categories* for more information).

Complaints and suggestions can also be classified as internal and external. Some external customer complaints are prevented by making corrections and redoing work before the customer receives it. The rework (doing it over) is an *internal* customer complaint and is the source of added cost to your business. Doing work over is a cost of quality (cost of nonconformance) that can be eliminated by *doing it right the first time.*

Feedback in the form of complaints provides excellent product and marketing information, and suppliers of products and services should listen to complaints with enthusiasm. Unfortunately, many businesses view customers who complain as problems and receive complaints with irritation, not enthusiasm. Complaints by definition are an indication that the customer's expectations are not being met. A customer who is willing to take the time to tell suppliers what was wrong with a product and/or service is a marketing asset. This information has great value in providing clues to understanding customer wants and needs, and ultimately benefits your operation. Customers who do *not* bother to complain are likely to just switch to another supplier.

Every customer complaint should be followed up promptly with action being taken to prevent recurrence. A timely response to a customer complaint or suggestion can lead to a stronger bond between you and the customer (similar to a weld commonly being stronger than the original steel it repairs).

> Feedback in the form of complaints provides excellent product and marketing information . . .

Some businesses post customer complaints (with action to prevent recurrence) and compliments in the workplace.

By setting zero complaint goals, you can actually create problems for your business. Remember that the marketplace is constantly changing. Consequently, customer needs and wants are dynamic, not static. Complaints help you remain competitive; they identify new market opportunities. Also, targeting zero complaints discourages complaint registration. Complaints are a fact of business. They will never be eliminated. Your goal, instead, should be to eliminate repeat complaints for the same product defect, service problem, documentation error, or transportation failure.

Do *not* target a specific level of complaints. There is no right level, whether complaints are running at 5 percent or 0.5 percent of shipments or service. Ensure that customers have a way to complain and that they receive a timely response.

Apply Quality Techniques and Prevention Tools

The problem-solving technique developed by the author's firm, called PMSA, is described here. PMSA is designed for preventing recurrence of existing defects. A problem-solving technique like PMSA should be applied to every defect, error, out-of-control point, and nonconformance of your current process, system, or method. Applying the techniques to find the root causes of problems does not mean that you should avoid using a "quick fix," (immediate action) to satisfy your internal or external customer. But the quick fix is a reflex action, like snatching your finger away from a hot stove. It's natural to do so, but then you need to discover and analyze the root cause. Quick fixes tend to offer only limited, Band-Aid® solutions. You can replace a defective product with a good one or perform services over and offer discounts to appease the customer, but those quick fixes won't prevent a recurrence.

Many organizations continue to solve Problem #27 over and over again. This kind of problem-solving inefficiency reduces profits, increases prices, and leaves customers with inferior quality products and services. Prevention systems like PMSA seek out the root cause of the problem, defect, or nonconformance, and eliminate it for good.

Example: The manager of a facility called in his staff and announced a new problem prevention program initiative to make quality products and learn to do it right the first time. Toward the end of the meeting, the manager asked for comments from the staff. They said this program did not involve them, they were already over-committed, and had no time for this program. Needless to say the facility manager had his way. The quality process was initiated. Six months later the staff was not spending precious time resolving

Problem #27 and managing rework but was practicing total prevention. Total prevention is applying quality techniques to be proactive and to work for a more productive and efficient operation.

The problem-solving system you implement should be objective, should focus on defining root causes, and should provide controls to ensure that action is being taken to prevent recurrence.

Your company quality policy (or mission statement) is the driving force for taking action. You have decided to improve quality, and you have formulated a policy that says, "quality pays; quality makes sense."

Apply the PMSA System to Problem Solving

The steps to preventing recurrence of defects for existing processes are as follows:

1. **P**roblem definition (stating the problem).
2. **M**easurement focus (gathering information and defining the root cause).
3. **S**olution (preventing recurrence).
4. **A**ction (implementing solutions to satisfy the customer) (quality milestone).

You can apply the problem-solving strategy as soon as the quality teams and feedback systems are in place. Preventing defects and problems is the payoff for your business.

Problem Definition. Defining the problem and stating it is harder than it sounds. Groups and teams have worked to define the root cause of a problem only to discover the problem was not stated or defined correctly. Ask yourselves the following questions: What will the process or system look like when it is working? How should this work? What quality triad components are not being satisfied?

Generally, problems of nonconformance belong in one of two categories:

1. The Type A problem is an actual deviation from verified (proven) performance: It is not as it should be.
2. The Type B problem is an actual deviation from expected (forecast) performance: It was never right to start with.

Regardless of the problem type, state the problem as a nonconformance (deviation from the quality triad components) and answer the standard questions: Who? What? When? Where? and How? The problem statement should be objective and focused on the customer (internal or external) needs. Too often managers blame people for problems, when in reality it is the system.

Example: Paul was not making his deliveries on time and customers were complaining. Is Paul the problem or is the delivery schedule the problem? To find the root cause, you must state the problem correctly: Paul's district customers, X, Y, and Z, are not receiving the product at the time it was promised.

A problem can surface at any time and at any place. Problems usually occur under the most inconvenient circumstances (Murphy's Law). The scope of the problem can be small or far-reaching, involving many departments and functions. The problem can involve internal or external products and services and a wide range of subject areas (for example, environmental, legal, safety, and corporate risk). Once you have identified the problem, you can apply the proper techniques and tools to define the root cause and take action to prevent recurrence.

Measurement Focus. Measurement and data gathering are the keys to validation of the problem and to pinpointing the root cause. The measurement step may reveal where this process differs from similar processes or from the process that was originally planned. It is not uncommon to find that the planned, documented process differs significantly from the actual process. Perhaps the documented process was unrealistic. Perhaps the operators lack training/education in the process.

> A problem can surface at any time and at any place.

Once you define the true process, it will be easier to define the root cause of your nonconformance. Flow chart techniques are excellent tools for understanding the steps or series of actions in a specific process (see *Section III — Help*). The measurement process helps narrow the scope of the problem to specific items that can contribute to the cause of the defect. The analysis step sorts the relevant from the nonrelevant and maintains a degree of objectivity.

Dr. W. Edwards Deming has divided the causes of defects and failures into two categories: common causes and special causes. *Common causes* are a result of the system and can be corrected only by management. *Special causes* are related to the individual process and must be corrected by the people operating the process. According to Deming, *85 percent or more* of the problems encountered result from common causes.

Quality management technology provides an entire arsenal of tools for evaluation of defects and errors. Your situation and your particular problem will dictate what tools need to be applied. The author strongly recommends that you use some statistical tool to verify the nature and existence of the problem and to help focus on the root cause. The author also recommends that you not overdo the use of statistical techniques. Why collect data for six months to construct control charts when a simple Pareto chart (see *Section III — Help*) will supply all the information you need?

Several of the most common measurement, classification, and sorting tools may be found in *Section III — Help*. They include the following:

- Histograms.
- Cause-and-effect diagrams (fishbone diagram).
- Flow diagrams.
- Pareto diagrams.
- Graphs and charts.
- Control charts and precontrol.
- Cost of quality.
- Brainstorming.
- Design of experiments (DOE).

Time and time again, management jumps the gun by defining the wrong problems and causes. There is good reason for solving problems quickly. Unsolved problems reduce corporate profits and absorb the organization's resources. Failure to define the *real problem* or *real causes* only adds to your organization's burden. You can ease that burden by appropriately using the statistical and problem-solving tools to get it right the first time.

Solution. A solution is not a solution unless it prevents recurrence of whatever caused the problem. In most cases the quick fix fails to address root causes. Taking action to *prevent recurrence* is the cornerstone of a more productive and efficient organization.

When you consider solutions and alternatives, *focus on the process*, not on individuals. If you simply increase your appraisal requirements for the desired output, you will not prevent recurrence. One cannot inspect quality into a product or service. The solution must prevent recurrence of the root cause(s). Several potential causes may have to be addressed. It may not be possible or practical to address all of them at once. In complex situations the team should define the solution that prevents recurrence of the primary root causes or the vital few as defined by a Pareto chart analysis.

Example: A continuous manufacturing production line experienced a quality excursion. The key variable was out of specification for two days. Several manual adjustments were made to an automatic metering device by the equipment operator. The metering device was the primary method of keeping the product variable at the correct level. Regardless of the adjustments, the quality control laboratory continued to report that the product was out of tolerance levels (specifications). Initially, several finger-pointing causes for the problem were presented by managers and supervisors such as the following:

- The operator was not following procedures and wasn't making the right adjustments.
- The operators were not responsive and just didn't care.
- The supervisor didn't take charge soon enough.

- The lab has a problem they're not telling us about and all the lab results are wrong.

All of this fingerpointing served no useful purpose and distracted the management focus of finding the root cause of the problem. Through trial and error techniques, a supervisor found out that the meter was partially clogged. The quick fix was to clean the meter. With the meter clean, the operation was back to normal in no time.

The plant manager called for a root-cause solution investigation to prevent recurrence. The following solutions were evaluated:

1. The operating procedures were not adequate to respond to the situation in a timely manner. Solution: Rewrite or modify the procedures.
2. A critical metering step such as this should have redundant control systems. Solution: Duplicate the metering control systems.
3. The operating unit has almost zero confidence in the laboratory results, and therefore did not respond to the problem fast enough. Solution: Increase the number of analyses.
4. The quality failure was a result of a clogged meter. Solution: Shut down the unit periodically and flush the meter. Solution: Install a filter before the meter to reduce the possibility of clogging. Solution: Double-check the quality of the material feeding the meter.
5. The meter clogged up because of the type of material it is handling. The meter is not suited for this application. Solution: Replace the meter with one that is fit for the application.

In this example, the quality action team had come up with several options, all of which would reduce the possibility that the quality failure would recur at the same magnitude. The action team reviewed the data, root causes, and solutions, and took action to implement numbers 1 and 5.

Actually, number 5 is the only solution that addressed the root cause. While the other solutions are more reactive in nature, by implementing the root-cause solution, the cause of the problem was eliminated. Was action taken to prevent recurrence? Yes!

Your solution to a problem must change or modify the system or process. Should you modify procedures? Set new requirements for materials or supplies? Install equipment that is fit for use? Evaluate a new technology? You may need to change your requirements in sampling or your appraisal methods. At all levels a certain amount of fear is likely to surround any change. Upper management fears that all the solutions will be in the category of building a new plant or facility. Lower and middle levels of an organization fear that there is no solution that will be supported if it costs money. The fact is, you are in business to make a profit. The quality management system is being implemented to secure a healthy future for the business. The solution(s) you define should:

- Prevent recurrence.
- Be economical.
- Be capable of being implemented in a reasonable time frame.

If appropriate, the action team may recommend more than one possible solution. If alternative solutions are feasible, your final decision for action and implementation may depend on your overall business requirements and expectations.

Management should be in a position to support the action teams and root-cause solutions. If upper management is not in a position to support root-cause solutions, then the organization's quality improvement process objectives and its commitment to those objectives should be reevaluated.

Action. Your next steps are to take action to prevent recurrence and to measure customer satisfaction. The action you take should fit into your normal business environment. The action may range from routine modification of a procedure or specification, to initiating a multi-million dollar capital expenditure involving several functions and requiring several levels of approval. This is when the cost of quality can be a particularly useful tool for management to prioritize and justify manpower and financial resources for projects.

> Management should be in a position to support the action teams and root-cause solutions.

COQ is expressed in terms of monetary benefits to provide a driving force for the organization to implement action. Your goal is to eliminate the cost of quality that will ultimately increase the organization's profits.

COQ is simply placing a dollar value on all the activities and tasks that will be eliminated if the job or output is performed right the first time. COQ can include (but is not limited to) the following:

- Scrap costs.
- Raw material losses.
- Extra paper work.
- Lost sales.
- Redoing.
- Replacement cost.
- Training costs.
- Out-of-service or downtime cost.
- Extra distribution costs.
- Yield losses.
- Inspection and testing cost.
- Complaint-handling cost.
- Rework.
- Extra inventory costs.

- Warranty expense.
- Rescheduling costs.
- Sorting.

COQ impacts a company's costs from two sources. The cost of prevention (appraisal) and the cost of failure (cost of correcting errors). The cost of appraisal is the cost of checking and inspecting products, services, paper work, shipments, tolerances, analysis, etc. The cost of correcting errors is the cost of reworking, returning, removing, redoing, etc. The American National Standard ANSI/ASQC Q94-1987 (published by ASQC) classifies COQ in the following categories:

- *Prevention costs* are the efforts to prevent failures such as testing, inspecting, and examination to assess if the quality is assured.
- *Failure costs* are either internal or external to the organization. The internal failure costs result when a product or service fails to meet quality requirement prior to delivery (i.e., reperforming the service, reprocessing, retest, rework, scrap, etc.). The external failure costs result when the product or service fails to meet quality requirements after delivery (i.e., customer service, returns, claims, complaint resolutions, warranties, etc.).

COQ reduces quality problems to the universal business yardstick — dollars. Currently, standard accounting systems record all the operating costs, but no provisions have been made to collect the costs under COQ. Therefore it is important to include the financial group in your quality improvement plans so it will be in full support of your goals and objectives. The standard accounting system is quick to charge a product or service for the fractional use of a piece of equipment or a human resource, yet very reluctant to credit a project for a fractional productivity improvement (i.e., 10 percent reduction of an operator's time or a 5 percent reduction in machine usage). This inflexibility has been a significant roadblock in preventing companies from building a bridge for continuous quality improvement.

Perhaps some day, the CEO will be reporting COQ reductions to stockholders and Wall Street as an indication of business competitiveness, stability, and future potential.

The quality master plan is not intended to detail the action process for your organization, but the process for taking action should be consistent with quality principles and goals. In the final analysis, the action taken should be neither more nor less than is needed to prevent recurrence of the problem and/or defect.

Once you have implemented corrective action, the action team (or one member) should follow up the root-cause solution to ensure that it produces customer satisfaction and defect-free products and services. Immediately after action is taken, it is not uncommon for the problem to recur due to special causes. An individual may not be following the new procedure. The new or modified equipment may be bypassed because employees lack training or confidence in the modification or change. If problems persist or if benefits of an idea have not materialized, then the root cause has not been identified nor has the full range of potential problems been anticipated.

Turn to *PMSA Root-Cause Solutions,* pages 104-111, and walk through a step-by-step example of the PMSA method and common quality tools and methods.

Implement Statistical Quality Control Methods

The use of statistics is one of the primary strategies for providing value to the customer. The application of statistical methods provides insight for management and results in a stable uniform process or system. Statistical methods can be applied to any product or service system.

The steps to implement the statistical quality control methods are as follows:

1. Select a statistical quality control method.
2. Implement statistical quality control pilot program (quality milestone).
3. Expand statistical quality control to remaining operations.
4. Bring processes "in control" and make them "capable" (quality milestone).
5. Qualify suppliers (quality milestone).

Statistical quality control (SQC) is a powerful and proven measurement tool for reducing variability in products and processes. Reduced variability means a more consistent and reliable product or service upon which the customer can depend. The application of SQC leads to a controlled process with little or no waste. The efficient use of resources (materials and personnel) will give your company the competitive edge it needs to survive in today's changing environment.

An asset of using SQC in the workplace is that it is an objective decision tool. No personalities or "shot-calling" is involved. SQC through the use of control charts can be applied to any business as the Deming/Japanese success has demonstrated. Deming is best known for his work in the early 1950s that revolutionized Japanese product quality. His philosophy and techniques were accepted and implemented by the captains of Japanese industry. The results of the 20-year rebuilding effort are self-evident in today's world economy.

A detailed explanation of SQC methods can best be covered by technically focused texts. In this section, I will limit my discussion to three concepts:

1. What does a control chart look like?
2. When is a process "in control"?
3. When is a process "capable"?

The selected key variable data are graphically represented on a horizontal chart shown in Figure 8. The data are plotted along an appropriate scale versus time. The key variable or attribute parameter could be percent activity, tolerance level in microns, time of delivery, etc. To illustrate the use of control charts let us assume that Figure 8 represents a graph of the times you arrived at work the last 20 days. The vertical axis represents actual arrival time and the horizontal axis represents each day of work attended. The data graph in Figure 8 gives you definitive historical information for the 20 days data was collected. Using statistical techniques, the sample data of 20 work days can accurately predict if your system (process) of transportation is in control and if your system is capable of getting you to work on time with 99.73 percent certainty.

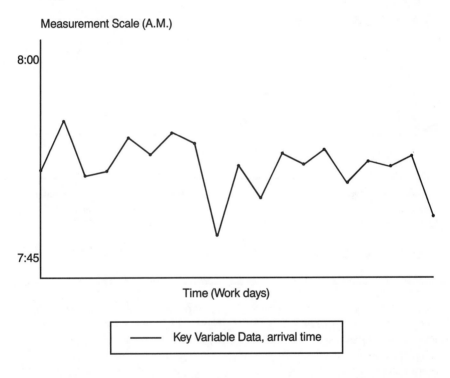

Figure 8   Trend Chart

Next, the upper and lower control limits (UCL, LCL) and the center line (CL) are calculated using statistical methods (Figure 9). If the key variable data are consistently within the upper and lower control limits, the process is considered to be "in control." Any point that falls outside the control limit lines is considered to be out of control — not stable — and requires action. Now you can see that your system (route and mode of transportation) is in control. You can statistically verify that you arrive at work within the upper

63

and lower control limits 99.73 percent of the time (out of control every one and one half years). However, you have not verified that you will be on time.

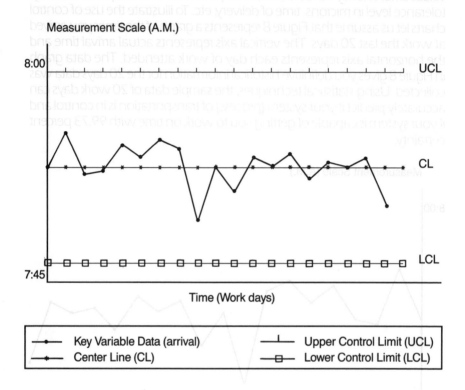

Figure 9   Control Chart with Process that Is In Control

The last concept of process capability is determined by adding the product or service upper and lower specification limits (USL, LSL) to the control chart (Figure 10). If the upper and lower control limits are within the specification limits (Figure 10) the process is considered "capable." The capable process will result in a product or service that will be within specifications at least 99.73 percent of the time. The example process (Figure 10) is "in control" and "capable." More good news for you: Your system (process) for getting to work is "in control" and "capable." You not only have a stable system but one that will allow you to arrive at work at the specified starting time. You want to share your newly found knowledge and agree to control chart the arrival time of a colleague. His chart looks very different from yours. Figure 11 shows a process that is not in control and is not capable.

Measurement Scale (A.M.)

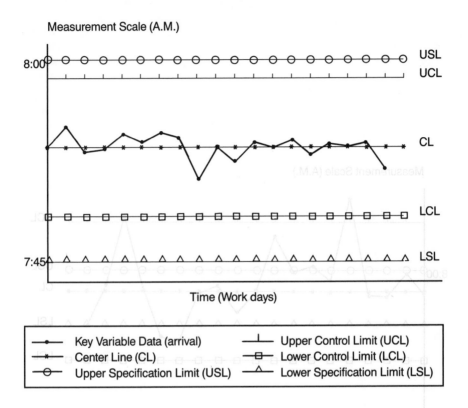

Figure 10   Control Chart that Is Capable

Note that the key variable points frequently fall outside the upper and lower control lines and that the specification limits are inside the control limits. In the case of arriving at work on time, your colleague should evaluate each out of control point and take corrective action to stabilize the system and bring it "in control." For example: (1) the colleague may need a consistent departure time, and (2) the route (system) to work may have frequent accidents and construction detours. Next, the colleague must modify the system (process) to make it "capable." For example, leave for work earlier.

Experience shows that most organizations who have been successful in improving quality have some type of SQC. However, experts differ regarding which SQC tools are the most effective and efficient for process control. Control charts developed by Walter Shewhart 60 years ago and popularized by Deming, have been widely credited with the turnaround in Japanese quality. Precontrol was founded by Frank Satherwaite 30 years ago and has been adopted by some U.S. organizations. Each organization must make its own decision on which methods to use based on its business environment and objectives.

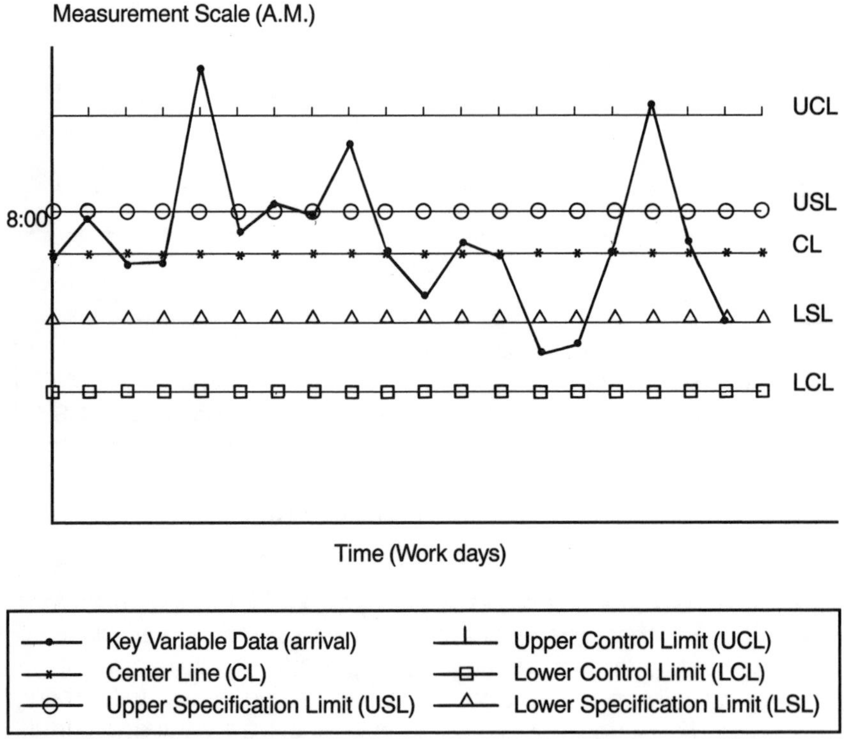
Measurement Scale (A.M.)
8:00
UCL
USL
CL
LSL
LCL
Time (Work days)
Key Variable Data (arrival)
Center Line (CL)
Upper Specification Limit (USL)
Upper Control Limit (UCL)
Lower Control Limit (LCL)
Lower Specification Limit (LSL)

Figure 11 Control Chart that Is Out of Control and Not Capable

Select a Statistical Quality Control Method

When selecting SQC tools and methods you should first consider their compatibility with your mainline business and with your management objective of meeting or exceeding business requirements. History indicates that statistical process control charts have had the most success with the mainline product or service of an organization (i.e., printers apply SQC to the printing press, automobile manufacturers apply SQC to the production line, chemical manufacturers apply SQC to the chemical product, delivery service company to delivery time, etc.). The use of process control charts for functions that support the mainline product or service has had limited success. Possibly this limited success can be attributed to insufficient resources, complexity of the operation, financial constraints, or diminishing returns.

Second, you need to select a method that is consistent with your business and operations strategy. Obviously, you are applying SQC to reduce variations in the process and to provide uniform, consistent products and/or services. But to what degree? To what requirements? A primary requirement of a business is to establish a process that is capable of consistently providing products and services that meet published specifications and standards (i.e., conformance to requirements). Normally, a business seeks to conform to government, societal, and competitive (customer) requirements that may involve legal, environmental, safety, and quality issues. But then what? Should you exceed those requirements, your decision to do so may be based on risk factors or company image. The justification for exceeding requirements should have some added value or payback to your organization.

Control charts are prevention tools to "do it right the first time". . .

The management focus of the quality master plan is to implement SQC to establish systems (processes) that are in control and capable (statistically conforming to customer requirements 99.73 percent of the time).

The most common SQC tool is the X-bar and R control chart, shown earlier. Control charts are prevention tools to "do it right the first time" instead of inspecting and doing it over. SQC is not just for manufacturing but should be applied to any process where constancy and uniformity are desirable. The only requirement for control charting is that the key variable or attribute is capable of being measured and that the desired properties can be represented numerically.

Select and Implement a Pilot SQC Process

As soon as several key people have been trained in SQC, select a process for implementation. Choose a process where a problem exists or where there is a considerable amount of rework. The pilot process will show immediate results for all to see and will provide hands-on experience before SQC is implemented on all processes. It is not uncommon for rework and off-grade to be cut by 50 percent in the first 12 months of implementation. People on the pilot project will be able to act as consultants for others in the organization who are implementing SQC in their departments.

Another good reason for the pilot program is that the SQC control chart cookbook methods are for standard ideal cases which seldom exist in the actual work environment.

For those not familiar with statistical process control techniques, the following steps must be implemented:

1. Collect and group data so that they can be treated statistically.
2. Develop and use control charts.
3. Identify special (assignable) causes and common causes of problems by statistical means.
4. Resolve the special causes. Special or assignable causes are unusual sources of variation. They can be addressed and corrected by the individual operating the process.
5. Management then executes and supports changes to the system to resolve (correct) common causes. Common causes are the most significant source of variation that influence all process observations such as poor design, obsolete equipment, poor procedures or methods (i.e., the type of problems that must be addressed by management).

You will need to ask the following questions:

• What are the key variables and attributes?
• Can they be quantified?
• Are the key variable results meaningful?
• Are samples representative?
• What is the lag time in the process?
• How do we handle out-of-control points?
• What if the control limits are greater than the specifications?

Expand SQC to Remaining Operations

Once the pilot project has been completed, continue to expand SQC application to all your processes. The only guideline for this step is to treat each process individually and to ensure that key variables and attributes are being measured. It would be counterproductive to praise one department because its process is in control and admonish another department for not being in control without knowing who is continually improving.

Bring Processes "In Control" and Make Them Capable

The purpose of SQC tools is to establish process stability (in control). The process stability is a result of detection and removal of special-cause sources of variation. The remaining variation is a result of common causes that are inherent in the process. The in-control, stable process has a characteristic set of upper and lower control limits. Next, determine if the in-control process is *capable* (consistently providing products or services within published specifications or standards). Process capability (Cp) indices are used to describe how well an in control process conforms to specification limits. A value of 1.0 would indicate that all the values (99.73 percent) would be in specification if the process were centered at the middle of the specification range. A capability of less than 1.0 would mean a reduction in common causes is necessary to be capable and in specification. In the case where we measured to work arrive time, your Cp would equal a number greater than one (i.e., Cp = 1.3), while your colleague would have a Cp of less than one (i.e., Cp = .75):

$$Cp = \frac{\text{Upper Specification} - \text{Lower Specification}}{6 \, \sigma \text{ (i.e., standard deviation)}}$$

The use of statistics and numbers in everyday life is not all that complicated. A little study will open up a new world of information about a company's process or system. After you apply SQC techniques, it will be easy to understand why certain products or services receive more complaints than others, why some projects have no added value to the business, and how to use the information to prioritize tasks and projects.

Example: The impurity content of a product was a specification property. BA Team Industries had been concerned about the impurity content of its product for years because the competitive product had a lower impurity content. There had been no customer complaints, yet research made an all-out effort to lower the impurity level to match competition. Implementation of SQC showed that the impurity content level was in control and the process was capable (i.e., the impurity level was consistent and uniform). Based on quality principles, BA Team Industries realized that impurity consistency was more important than the actual level. It was obvious that the 30 percent of the research budget being spent on impurity reduction could be better spent on more important issues. In fact, the plant stopped measuring impurity content except for statistical verification that the process was in control and capable.

69

Qualification of Suppliers

It will be costly and difficult to bring the process in control and to supply a product or service that consistently meets customer expectations if the inputs (raw materials, service equipment, procedures, and training) for the process are not in control. Quality management requires suppliers to demonstrate that the products and services they supply are in control and capable. Suppliers should be notified of quality plans ahead of time so there are no surprises. It is better to have a few excellent suppliers of products and services than several wide-range suppliers. Here, *you* are the customer, and you should expect to receive a product or service that is consistent and fit for its intended use.

Choosing a supplier that has implemented total quality management will reduce your appraisal cost, improve process stability, eliminate raw materials and supplies as root causes of problems, and increase customer satisfaction. You can realize greater utility of products and services by establishing clear requirements and a relationship of continuous quality improvement. A company can afford neither the high cost of raw material appraisal nor the domino effect on the process when out-of-control products or services are supplied.

Some key performance outputs that you may expect the supplier to provide include the following:

- Quality materials, supplies, and services that are uniform, consistent, in control, and capable.
- On-time delivery/performance.
- Accurate invoicing/billing.
- Timely market information.
- Opportunities (ideas) for cost savings.

You may want to develop a system for ranking your suppliers in order of your confidence in their ability to meet all requirements all the time. The classification can range from the most confident class to least confident or nonapproved class. The steps for qualifying supplier location and materials follow:

1. Assess your requirements and wants.
2. Have the supplier complete a customer information survey and specification verification.
3. Review the supplier's past performance.
4. Test the supplier's materials, products, or services.
5. Establish internal customer systems for monitoring and certification.
6. Review (audit) the supplier's quality management system(s).

Some typical factors that affect the classification of product suppliers are shown in *Section III — Help*. These qualification criteria are limited to the conformance of product requirements, process control, and inspection and testing. The criteria factors can be easily expanded to encompass such factors as quality management systems, testing/analysis control, purchasing, distribution and storage systems, corrective action, training, and internal audit results.

In many cases the supplier must satisfy several customers within one organization. The receiving customer(s) within the organization may represent purchasing, manufacturing (operations), technology, quality assurance, etc. All receiving customers should be included in the evaluation of suppliers.

GOAL IV: ACHIEVE CONTINUOUS IMPROVEMENT

Quality improvement is continuous and never-ending. Goals I through III provide the foundation or framework for the quality improvement process. Goal IV provides for maintaining, improving, and expanding your quality efforts by establishing an ongoing system for changing the way you and your employees conduct your business.

The implementation of Goal IV, *achieve continuous improvement,* is supported by four strategies, each of which has several steps (Figure 12). These strategies are to:

- Establish a quality education system.
- Form audit systems.
- Integrate total prevention.
- Integrate total quality management.

Continuous improvement requires that quality principles be constantly reinforced through ongoing communication and exchange of ideas throughout your organization.

Your timing in executing Goal IV will depend on your customized implementation plan and the resources available to you. The quality schedule plan (see *Section III — Help*) strategies of Goal IV are integrated with the other three goals to avoid confusion and to provide a logical sequence. Several Goal IV strategies (e.g., auditing a quality management system) require the establishment of a quality management system before they can be executed. However, your specific plan may require early implementation of external supplier audits to upgrade and control critical raw materials and supplies.

73

Objective: Change the organization culture (attitude) to a total quality way of management to improve competitiveness (survival) and to prosper.

Goal	Strategy
I. Integrate and promote quality management	Commit to a quality policy
	Market total quality and team building concepts
	Demonstrate management commitment
	Involve all levels
II. Build an organization responsive to customer needs and wants	Integrate quality into the business organization
	Educate the organization in quality concepts and methods
III. Consistently provide value to the customer	Build a foundation for improvement
	Apply quality techniques and tools for prevention
	Implement statistical quality control methods
IV. Achieve continuous improvement	Establish a quality education system
	Form audit systems
	Integrate total prevention
	Integrate total quality management

Establish a quality education system

Form audit systems
Integrate total prevention

	The importance of being proactive
	The DEVSA prevention system

Integrate total quality management

	Organization structure
	Job description/performance
	Feedback
	Procedures and standards
	Quality management plan

(Also refer to plan schedule in *Section III — Help*)

Figure 12   Goal IV Detail Chart

Establish a Quality Education System

You will need an ongoing program of training to reinforce your new way of doing business, but the scope of this program will evolve as you implement your quality process. Your strategic objective is to change your intrinsic organizational culture to a quality management style.

Continuous emphasis on quality education will help you:

- Uphold your company's quality policy.
- Stay abreast of new quality management techniques and technologies.
- Prevent backsliding to the old ways that didn't work.

You will need three kinds of quality education programs. The first two are straightforward and easily grasped; the third is more subtle but has great importance.

First, you need an education program that involves everyone already in your business. This program should provide ongoing training in the use of quality improvement tools as well as a forum for the exchange of concerns and suggestions regarding quality. Employee quality meetings should be held once a month and should last at least an hour.

If your company currently conducts monthly safety meetings, you can use these as a pattern for organizing your quality meetings. Possibly you can combine the two functions. After all, safety education focuses on the prevention of injuries; quality education focuses on the prevention of defects by *doing it right the first time*. Some topics for quality through prevention might include the following:

- Problem analysis techniques.
- Quality measurement tools.
- Cost of quality in the department.
- Modeling the process.
- Getting customer feedback.
- Statistical quality control.
- Identifying customers and their expectations.
- Customer audits and what they mean.

The second area of quality education involves orienting and indoctrinating new employees. Unfortunately, most formal business education courses lack training in quality awareness. New employees need to learn the rules of the road in your organization — what you, the employer, expect in terms of quality, just as they need information about working hours, health benefits, and other policies of your business. A goal of The Quality Master Plan is to provide an introduction to common quality improvement elements and principles.

The last but most important aspect of quality education is making quality a part of every meeting. The quality attitude must not be relegated to once-a-month meetings. It must underlie all your business activities, whether they be sales, customer service, manufacturing, maintenance, finance, or distribution.

Form Audit Systems

Quality audits are measurement tools that assist management and employees in gauging the status of the quality improvement process. Audits evaluate how consistently the business — every department, every function — is meeting customers' expectations and needs. The American National Standard ANSI/ASQC Q1-1986 (published by ASQC) defines a quality system audit as

> . . . A documented activity performed to verify, by examination and evaluations of objective evidence, that applicable elements of the quality system are appropriate and have been developed, documented, and effectively implemented in accordance and in conjunction with specified requirements.

Audits can be valuable tools, but they can also be a drain on your resources. A few years ago, audits were relatively simple and limited to a few dozen pages. Today, internal audits may consist of detailed manuals more than 100 pages long which may actually increase overhead costs (appraisal costs). These huge manuals require people to write them, people to keep them up to date, people to interpret them, and people to execute the audits. I recommend the KISS principle: the *keep it simple system*. Apply the KISS principle to prevent adding personnel, wasting resources, and multiplying hassles.

Organizational (internal) audits may be generated from three sources:

- The customer (external customer audits).
- Headquarters (internal customer audits).
- Individual units conducting self-assessments.

Externally, you may conduct audits to assess your suppliers' capacity to supply quality products and services and conform to contractual requirements. The type of audit that is appropriate varies with your quality objective and the department, product, or service involved. In its 1987 *Quality Assurance for the Chemical and Process Industries — A Manual of Good Practices*, ASQC lists four basic types of audits:

- *Good manufacturing practice* (GMP) audits are performed to determine compliance to documented manufacturing practices and procedures.

77

In a broad sense, the audit can be used to determine whether a manufacturing process is able to control the product or service it produces.

- *Good laboratory practices* (GLP) audits assess the ability of a testing laboratory to provide accurate results.
- *Quality systems audits* determine the existence, structure, and health of the quality program (process) in a company. The quality systems audit may include GMP, GLP, and evaluation of all support and manufacturing or service systems.
- *Specific product/service/process audits* start with the raw material selection for a process and follow every step of the process until the final product is shipped. The audit measures continuity, uniformity, and communication within the process. Similarly, a service audit starts with the inputs required to perform a service and follows every step of the process or system until the service is completed.

Audit standards and guidelines are available from several industry sources. Industry associations and societies are good resources for audit information. Specifically, ASQC has developed a set of industry standards as a guide to aid the manufacturer, the consumer, and the general public. These American National Standards are listed in *Section III — Help*.

Keep the audits simple, minimize the number of audits, and use outside resources when practical. Using the resources of specialized consultants offers the following advantages:

- The consultant has already designed and developed an audit or checklist; you need not do so.
- You need not build up internal resources to develop and administer the audit.
- Audit ratings are reported by an independent, unbiased third party.
- Customers who need verification of supplier quality improvement may accept the independent audits, relieving the supplier organization of duplication of effort.
- The service consultants training, experience, certification, and professionalism will avoid the pitfalls and internal hassles that can develop when audits are poorly executed and reported.

Integrate Total Prevention into Your Organization

Integrating total prevention means applying quality improvement techniques and tools to opportunities and activities throughout your organization. Use the DEVSA prevention technique described in the following pages to develop new products or perform new services *right the first time.* Just as an economic evaluation of new projects is routine, so should there be a quality evaluation and sensitivity study of new initiatives. You can apply DEVSA to eliminate appraisals, dehassle your organization, and eliminate work that has no added value. DEVSA is a customer-focused, prevention-based proactive approach for implementing new initiatives and verification of existing systems.

The Importance of Being Proactive

Organizations are forever concerned about future risks and opportunities, yet they tend to be reactive rather than proactive. Each opportunity has its own level of business risk and uncertainty. The DEVSA prevention method concentrates on reducing the level of uncertainty by managing for success *(doing it right the first time).*

You can enhance your chances of success with any business initiative by making full use of your current knowledge and information. This does not mean that you should use prevention techniques to delay acting on the opportunity. You should use them to provide a clear focus for evaluating and implementing your plans.

The DEVSA prevention system is designed to focus on uncertainties that can be altered by taking action.

> Organizations
> are forever
> concerned
> about future
> risks . . .

Example: INC Corporation focused all of its resources on developing and manufacturing a new product without fully understanding customer expectations of product performance. Yet one customer's negative reaction represented 50 percent of the entire market for the product. When the new product did not meet INC's mega-customer's requirements, INC tried different manufacturing methods until three years' product inventory had accumulated. It was all too obvious that INC's mega-customer would not adopt the INC product in the near term. In response, INC developed a new, refocused marketing program that created a profitable market niche based on INC product attributes, but with much lower volumes than originally forecast. Had INC evaluated its customers' needs and requirements before embarking on production, three years' wasted effort could have been avoided.

The DEVSA Prevention System

The DEVSA system consists of the following five steps:

1. **D**efine.
2. **E**valuate.
3. **V**alidate.
4. **S**ystematize.
5. **A**ct.

Define the Action or Activity. Your business initiatives — both the opportunity and the activity — must be clearly defined in an *opportunity statement.* Define the proposed action (who, what, when, and where) and the reasons for undertaking it. Correcting defects of existing systems is not what business initiatives are about: They are about developing new systems to increase business and improve the competitive strength of your organization. The initiative could consist of developing and introducing a new product or service, or installing a new facility or computerized order entry system.

Evaluate the Customer's Requirements and Expectations. Your customer is the internal or external receiver of the product or service you are considering. What does your customer want? Answering this question in detail ensures that customers will use your new product or service. Don't evaluate by asking yourself what your customers want: *Ask the customer!* Involve all the customers who will be affected by your initiative. Categorize the responses: Which of your customers' wants and requirements are controllable? Which are not controllable? Then sort the customers' wants according to value and potential impact on cost. It is not unusual to discover requirements you had not anticipated.

Not all project requirements are customer related. Suppliers, including those in your own organization, can also impose limitations. Estimate and validate supplier requirements such as capital funds, raw materials, equipment, and response time.

Validate the Quality Triad Components. Does the product or service add value? Will it meet customer needs and wants? Is it needed — now? You need to validate your initiative in terms of the quality triad. Every business initiative is based on certain assumed requirements and expectations. Use the following questions to sort the real requirements from the presumed:

- What is the objective of the project/operation/activity?
- Are the requirements valid? Why?
- What potential opportunities and risks accompany each requirement or expectation?
- Does the requirement have added value to the customer and to your organization?

- Are there alternatives?
- Is this required now, all at once, or can it be done in phases?
- Does this plan make the most sense?
- Are the suppliers capable of meeting imposed requirements?

Systematize to Meet Customer Requirements. Success requires systemization. This step is analogous to defining a root-cause solution by developing a system for preventing defects, errors, and nonconformances. In this case, however, you are preventing a potential problem rather than defining a solution to an existing defect — *doing it right the first time* instead of increasing your inspection and appraisal costs.

The following tips might help you develop and implement a system:

- Conduct a quality assessment as the project develops to ensure that it meets primary requirements.
- Consider what problems could develop from the new system.
- Identify contingency plans to minimize risk related to noncontrollable requirements or expectations.

Act to Implement Quality Systems. Consistently providing quality products and services requires action. This step includes normal business procedures for securing approvals and taking action. After your project, operation, or activity has been implemented, keep your awareness open to changes in the process or in the environment that might create a similar problem with a different root cause.

> Consistently providing quality products and services requires action.

Neither DEVSA nor any problem prevention system can guarantee that your project, operation, or activity will be defect free. DEVSA can reduce the uncertainty of future events to a manageable level.

The same DEVSA steps can be used to verify the need and value of existing systems.

Example: A business manager, in a team meeting, complained to the logistics manager about a lack of communication concerning distribution costs and efficiency data. The information was needed for effective marketing and pricing action. The logistics manager reported that all requested information was contained in his 30-page monthly report sent to the business manager. The logistics manager stated that he would supply any needed additional information if the business manager would justify the additional expenses. At this juncture it would not be unusual for the investigative process to stop, because of organizational issues (business manager and logistics manager reporting to different vice presidents) or because any justification could be easily refuted.

The business manager was not satisfied that it should cost more to get the information she wanted so she decided to apply the DEVSA steps. The issue (or problem) is that the business manager is not receiving the information she expects and needs. The business manager suggested that a representative from her department and the logistics department meet to evaluate the quality triad components. The results of the meeting verified that:

- The information *was* needed by the business unit.
- The required information *was* contained in the report.
- Most of the information contained in the report had no added value or utility for the business unit.
- The required data were in a format that was not easily disseminated to nor understood by business unit personnel.

The DEVSA steps led to the report's reduction from 30 pages to five pages (value added information only) and the required information reported on a market segment basis compared to the previous unit basis. The organization saved money. The organization benefited by:

- Satisfying the internal customer (business manager).
- Reducing report publication cost.
- Increasing productivity of the logistics department.
- Improving the cost-effectiveness of business performance because the monthly information could be easily applied to market decisions.

How many reports go directly from the top of your desk to the bottom of the circular file? Do your subordinates need or require all the information they receive? There are numerous cases where existing management systems are not adding value. They may have an historical basis but no value basis. The following are some examples of this:

- Filed and cataloged information and reports that are never used again. (Note: You may want to isolate and validate legal and regulatory requirements.)
- Duplicate filing and cataloging.
- Reports that are of no use to the receiver (e.g., reports that are internally rather than customer-focused).
- Inspection or verification procedure of a product or service problem that has already been corrected.

Integrate Total Quality Management

This final strategy addresses management systems — policies and practices that must be changed or redeveloped to reflect ongoing, never-ending quality improvement. You should expand the scope of this quality strategy to encompass every management system that is not consistent with your business objectives.

Your management duties are planning, organizing, directing, and controlling. When these duties are properly executed, profitability increases and organizational objectives are achieved. Management plans, organizes, directs, and controls by decisions. These decisions affect the organizational structure, directives, hiring practices, performance appraisals, company policies, standard operating practices, job descriptions, job specifications, work flow, company geographical dispersion, strategic plans, quality plans, business plans, and resource allocation. Management simply defines and manages the system or process. The management system is based on certain assumptions and business principles. Historically, business principles have fostered the following ideas: (1) volume of output is preferred over quality, (2) quality costs, and (3) big is better. In light of new management technology (i.e., the quality improvement process), the existing business strategies, company policies, and unit standards need to be reexamined.

Steps for total quality management integration include the following:

- Clarify and communicate the mission of the organization *clearly.*
- Establish policies and guidelines consistent with quality principles.
- Apply the prevention style of management and limit short-term thinking and quick fixes to specific, immediate customer needs.
- Establish team concepts for achieving improved business performance.
- Support teams by providing the tools (quality education) and resources (quality professionals and allocation of time) to accomplish quality objectives.
- Incorporate quality management objectives into the marketing and operating strategy.
- Include current quality objectives in job descriptions and individual performance requirements.
- Foster a continuous improvement style of management versus a "once-and-done" mentality.

Organizational Structure

Your organizational structure communication lines should be crisp and clear, minimizing the hierarchical levels while maintaining a customer orientation. Since the best way to improve competitiveness and increase profits is through customer satisfaction, your organization should be structured to respond to customer needs and wants to prevent the many barriers that get in the way of continuous improvement. The ideal situation is for *one* manufacturing unit to produce product for *one* marketing group to sell in *one* market segment. This is seldom a reality.

Some companies are organized to meet internal functional objectives (e.g., the most efficient transportation department or the most up-to-date and detailed financial data reporting) without considering the flow of work and its response to customer (market) needs and wants. The manager of a facility that provides several products to several business units normally does not have the time to fully understand the needs of all customers. Management decisions may take the path of least resistance, or they may be a function of internal corporate survival requirements. Conflicts easily develop between schedule, cost, and quality. In the case of a single facility that houses multiple plants, the customer conflicts can be minimized if each plant (unit) manager interfaces with the respective business unit. The author recommends a strong customer response structure for multiple plant/product facilities. The diagram shown in Figure 13 integrates functional and customer-focused structures.

This diagram oversimplifies most organizational structures, but consideration must be given to maintaining a customer focus and integrating customer quality triad components. You can apply the same thought process to both the internal customer (department serving department) and the external customer.

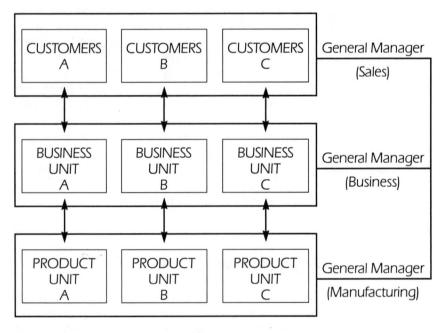

Figure 13   Customer-Focused Structure

Manufacturing companies are not the only ones that exclude customers by their functional organizational structure. Service companies can become so specialized that they lose sight of satisfying the customer's quality triad components (requirements, expectations, and value). Possibly you have called an insurance company, bank, or department store and had your call transferred from one department to another. I call this "telephone monopoly" because the caller is transferred to several different departments and usually ends at the starting point, without any answers (and does not pass "Go" and certainly does not collect $200).

Example: Paul was at a hospital and needed some information on hospital care from five different insurance companies in order to make an important decision concerning the health and care of a relative. He was at a pay telephone with the insurance policies and the insurance companies' telephone numbers. Three of the five insurance companies hassled Paul endlessly with multiple transfers, placing him on hold, directing him to other locations, recommending that he call back later, or with promises that someone would get back to him soon. This type of merry-go-round (telephone monopoly) indicates that these companies were not organized to respond to the customer. Their structured specialization efforts did not encompass the customer's needs and wants.

Your organizational structure may have a market, product, or functional bases, but in all cases at all levels, it must have a customer focus.

> **The top quality executive does not need to be a quality professional.**

The quality administrator of your company should have unhindered access to senior management. The title of the top quality administrator should be consistent with his or her peers (quality vice president or quality director). The top quality executive does not need to be a quality professional. Possibly, you can combine the top quality post with other prevention-based functions such as training, safety, and regulatory affairs.

In summary:

- Establish clear lines of communication and authority.
- Be customer-focused.
- Provide the top quality administrator with unhindered access to senior management.

Job Descriptions/Performance

For every job there should be a job description. The job description summarizes the job authority, responsibility, duties, specific task requirements, and job reports. The job description of each subordinate should complement that of his or her superior to ensure smooth flow of work toward company objectives. Each job contains a set of qualifications that detail the education experience, training, and special attributes necessary to be successful.

Your business quality objectives should be incorporated into every job description and each individual performance review. When you initiate the quality improvement process certain employees will readily adopt the new business principles. Their acceptance is based on the belief that they will be rewarded for changing their behavior and that quality makes sense. However, the majority of your employees will not change their habits until quality requirements are stipulated in the job description and specified in their individual performance reviews. Your job descriptions and performance reviews are two of the most important management tools for directing and controlling the activities of the organization.

Example: Purchasing agents and buyers have been required to purchase raw materials and supplies for the lowest price possible and rewarded for doing so. In terms of performance, the most important criterion has been the price variance (favorable or unfavorable) of the materials the buyer has purchased. A favorable price variance means the buyer has purchased materials for less than was anticipated or budgeted. If a buyer's activities result in a favorable price variance, he or she is doing a good job. If his or her activities result in a negative price variance, he or she is doing a poor job. It is a simple straightforward system: The problem is that it makes no provision for the total impact of purchasing decisions on the organization.

It is rare that the total financial consequences of a purchasing decision are reflected in an individual buyer's performance review. Consequently the buyer seeks every opportunity to generate a positive price variance, which may include decisions to: (1) purchase outdated equipment solely because (s)he can claim a 10 percent favorable variance, or (2) persuade manufacturing to use slightly off-specification materials because of a 20 percent discount, or (3) qualify poor quality suppliers because the alternatives would result in an unfavorable price variance. From the buyer's perspective it would be heresy to pay more for a material than is absolutely necessary as long as it can be used. But what are the criteria for what is usable? If the criteria are that the material be consistent and uniform, and meet requirements 100 percent of the time, then the above alternatives would not be pursued. The "money saving strategies" described above will, in my experience, cost the company money far in excess of any purchase price savings.

> Your job descriptions and performance reviews are two of the most important management tools . . .

In addition to the product specific criteria, buyers and purchasing agents must contractually require suppliers to implement a quality management process to ensure continuous improvement. Restating the buyer's job performance requirements to include quality objectives will not only validate the company quality mission on an individual basis, but will also provide supportive interaction and synergy with other departments within the organization.

Every employee, not just the purchasing agent, is affected by the quality improvement process. Job requirements that provide a customer focus affect every action of every person in the organization. How often, as a customer, have you called a supplier's organization and been made to feel that you are an inconvenience when in fact, you, as a customer, are the very purpose of the supplier's work? A satisfied customer is the key to the success of any business or organization. Every employee (from custodian to president) is an ambassador for customer satisfaction. The sales clerk, switchboard operator, receptionist, or accounting clerk can be responsive to the customer *or* can treat the customer as a necessary evil who is time away from more important concerns. The change in management style — the change in how the corporate objectives are achieved — must be reflected in *each* employee's work habits and attitude.

In summary, you need to do the following:

- Review all job descriptions and qualifications to ensure they are clear and conform to the quality improvement principles . . . a new way of doing business.
- Incorporate quality objectives into individual performance requirements.

Feedback

A work activity is a series of steps that lead to a desired result — in other words, a process. Every process has an input and an output. Total quality management requires that every process contain feedback loops for continuous quality improvement (Figure 14). Feedback keeps every system competitive and responsive to the customer quality triad components. The customer may be the (internal) recipient of the monthly financial report or the (external) recipient of the organization's product or service.

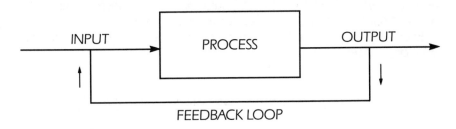

Figure 14   Customer Feedback (Internal and External)

Procedures and Standards

Your existing standards and procedures will create barriers to quality unless they incorporate the quality improvement process principles. One company actually burned its procedures book and started fresh. I do not think such drastic action is necessary, but it is advisable to review existing procedures to ensure that they conform to quality business objectives. In one case, the review of order-taking procedures revealed that: (1) the written procedures did not agree with what was actually being done, (2) what was practiced did not take advantage of newly installed computer technology systems, (3) the procedure was basically a flow chart for paper work, (4) the procedure did not focus on quality (customer satisfaction) objectives, and (5) order-taking inconsistencies caused several customer complaints.

Quality Management Plan

Another management responsibility is planning. This book and published quality standards (such as *ANSI/ASQC Q94-1987* published by ASQC) are excellent starting points for developing a customized quality management plan and or quality manual. In addition, your quality principles and company quality objectives must be incorporated into your strategic and business plans. The new way of doing business by doing it right the first time, by meeting customer quality triad components, must be amplified to every company function.

Your organization cannot achieve continuous quality improvement unless every employee understands management's expectations and is rewarded for outstanding performance. Managers, executives, and supervisors must reinforce a quality management style every day. Every contact with an employee is an opportunity to educate, and every decision is an opportunity to achieve improvement. Unless you reward employees who practice prevention and build for the future, the quick-fix, crisis-management mentality will gain control. As in nature, balance is the key to survival.

Every day, ask yourself the following four questions about any problem, decision, concern, or situation:

Quality Improvement Questions (Quality IQ)

1. Who are our customers (internal and external)?
2. How does this meet the quality triad components?
3. What have we done to ensure we do it right the first time?
4. What action have we taken to prevent recurrence?

Repeated use of the Quality IQ will reinforce the behavioral changes that are necessary for continuous quality improvement in your company or business. The questions will help prioritize problems, provide customer focus, and support taking action to prevent recurrence.

Finally, each organization must develop its own unique quality improvement plan and continually update it to achieve total quality management. *The Quality Master Plan* was created to increase your awareness of quality as a continuous process, to assist you in successfully implementing that process, and to stimulate a sense of renewal in your organization and its people.

Final Remark

"There was a law of life so cruel and so just,
Which demanded that one must grow
Or else pay for remaining the same."

Norman Mailer

SECTION III
HELP

EXAMPLES OF ACTION LIST

**MANUFACTURING
MATERIALS MANAGEMENT
SERVICE MANAGEMENT
MARKETING**

MANUFACTURING

1. DEVELOP OPERATING PROCEDURES THAT RESPOND TO KEY VARIABLE DEVIATIONS.

2. DEFINE KEY PROCESS VARIABLE TARGETS AND RANGES.

3. PROMOTE QUALITY.

4. PROVIDE QUALITY AWARENESS AND STATISTICAL QUALITY CONTROL EDUCATION.

5. DEFINE A REPRESENTATIVE SAMPLING SYSTEM.

6. REPORT KEY QUALITY PARAMETERS, VARIABLES, AND ATTRIBUTES ON PRODUCTION REPORTS.

7. PREPARE PROCEDURE FOR EQUIPMENT SHUT DOWN AND START UP.

8. EVALUATE ANALYTICAL TESTS AND METHODS FOR CAPABILITY AND PRECISION.

9. VALIDATE PRODUCT SPECIFICATIONS (MANUFACTURING/SALES/CUSTOMER).

10. VERIFY HANDLING AND LOADING REQUIREMENTS (QUALITY TRIAD COMPONENTS).

11. DEVELOP TREND CHARTS.

12. UPGRADE CONTROL OF KEY VARIABLES/PARAMETERS/ATTRIBUTES.

MATERIALS MANAGEMENT

1. VERIFICATION OF SPECIFICATIONS.

2. ALTERNATIVE SUPPLIERS AND AVAILABILITY.

3. SPECIFICATION RANGES AND TARGETS.

4. VENDOR CERTIFICATE OF ANALYSIS OR STATISTICAL PROCESS CONTROL CHARTS.

5. RECEIPT VALIDATION.

6. APPRAISAL COST AND REQUIREMENTS EVALUATION.

7. REJECTION AND INVESTIGATION.

SERVICE MANAGEMENT

1. DEFINE KEY SERVICE PARAMETER TARGETS AND LEVEL OF VARIATION:
   - Primary service.
   - Auxiliary (required extra service).
   - Non-obligatory (service expected by customers).

2. EVALUATE QUOTES COMPARED TO ACTUAL CHARGES.

3. TARGET A RESPONSE TIME TO SERVICE REQUESTS AND MEASURE PERFORMANCE.

4. DEFINE CUSTOMER HASSLES:
   - Unnecessary and/or complicated forms.
   - Waiting for service.
   - Too many rules and procedures.

5. DEFINE INTERNAL HASSLES:
   - Rework and redo.
   - Too much paperwork and duplication.

6. VERIFY COMMITMENT TO THE CUSTOMER(S):
   - Time.
   - Place.
   - Cost.

7. DEFINE CUSTOMER COMMUNICATION REQUIREMENTS:
   - Changes in service.
   - Understanding service.
   - Understanding terms and conditions.

8. IMPLEMENT STATISTICAL QUALITY CONTROL FOR KEY SERVICES:
   - Define measurement system.
   - Publish standards.

MARKETING

1. **DEFINE PROCEDURES (GUIDELINES) TO CONFORM TO CUSTOMER RESPONSE TIME REQUIREMENTS FOR:**
   - **Complaints and complaint resolution.**
   - **Return goods authorization and credit.**
   - **Competitive price requests.**

2. **REPORT AND MEASURE DEFECTS AND NONCONFORMANCE (E.G., CUSTOMER CPR PROGRAM).**

3. **DEFINE SALESFORCE EXPECTATIONS (EQUIPMENT, COMMUNICATIONS, SUPPORT, ETC.).**

4. **PROMOTE QUALITY (E.G., CUSTOMER PRESENTATION AND PRODUCT LITERATURE).**

5. **ESTABLISH REQUIREMENTS FOR NEW DEVELOPMENTAL PRODUCTS AND SERVICES.**

6. **DEFINE NEW CUSTOMER ORIENTATION AND INFORMATION NEEDS.**

7. **EVALUATE EFFECTIVENESS AND REQUIREMENTS OF THE PRODUCT SAMPLE AND/OR THE SERVICE TRIAL PROGRAM.**

CUSTOMER CPR COMPLAINT CATEGORIES
(Complaints/Problems/Response)

COMPLAINT CATEGORIES AND TYPES

PRODUCT OR SERVICE:

- Performance (did not work or do what it was supposed to do).
- Specification or standards (was not provided in accordance with specifications and standards or procedures).

DISTRIBUTION:

- Product or service not on time.
- Wrong product shipped.
- Wrong service performed.
- Wrong product quantity or package.
- Product damaged or lost.

DOCUMENTATION/COMMUNICATION:

- Pricing (over/under charge).
- Allowances/freight.
- Complaint/request response time too long (waiting complaints).

QUALITY MANAGEMENT TOOLS

BRAINSTORMING GUIDELINES
FLOW CHARTS
CAUSE-AND-EFFECT DIAGRAMS
PARETO CHARTS

BRAINSTORMING GUIDELINES

PURPOSE: TO GENERATE IDEAS IN A GROUP.

- Everyone gets to participate.
- Everyone can comment during their turn or later.
- As many ideas as possible are given.
- No arguing, criticism, or evaluation during the session.
- Ideas are ranked and sorted (category, importance, priority, benefit, cost, impact, time, etc.).

FLOW CHARTS

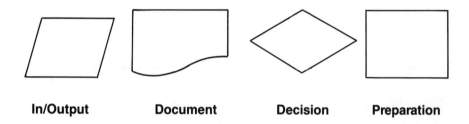

| In/Output | Document | Decision | Preparation |

PURPOSE: A TOOL TO DESCRIBE A PROCESS OR SYSTEM.

- Define the process steps by brainstorming or form a reference document.
- Sort the steps as they occur in the process.
- Place a box or the appropriate flow chart symbol around each process step.
- Evaluate the steps for completeness, efficiency, and possible problems.

(See example, page 106.)

CAUSE-AND-EFFECT DIAGRAMS

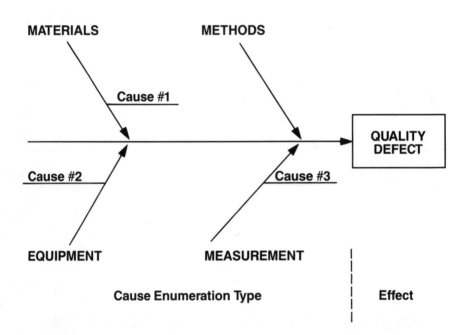

PURPOSE: A TOOL TO IDENTIFY AND SORT CAUSES OF A PROBLEM.

- Draw the diagram as shown above.
- Define the quality defect, characteristic, or problem and place in the box on the right.
- Define the main causes of the problem and group according to the four cause areas.
- Identify the most likely causes and collect data to validate.

(See example, page 107.)

PARETO CHARTS

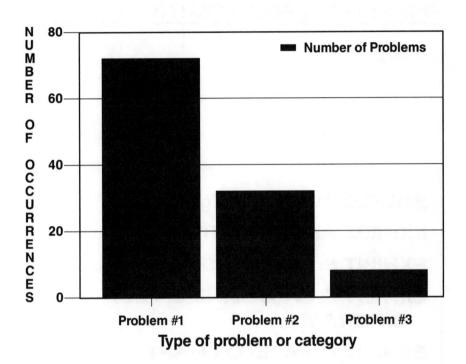

PURPOSE: TO RANK PROBLEMS/CAUSES/CATEGORIES TO IDENTIFY THE MOST IMPORTANT.

- List problems/causes/categories and the corresponding frequency of occurrence.
- Sort data by the highest frequency first and place on the chart, as above.
- The data will graphically show which problems are the most important and which to work on first.

(See example, page 108.)

103

PMSA ROOT-CAUSE SOLUTIONS

BACKGROUND INFORMATION

EXHIBIT A: ACTION ITEM LIST

EXHIBIT B: SIMPLIFIED FLOW CHART

EXHIBIT C: CAUSE-AND-EFFECT DIAGRAM

EXHIBIT D: PARETO CHART

EXHIBIT E: BENEFITS, COST OF QUALITY CALCULATION SHEET

EXHIBIT F: PMSA DISCUSSION

SUMMARY

BACKGROUND INFORMATION

Goods Returned Due to Improper Identification. The B.A. Team Industries manufacturing facility produces several products that are all packaged on the same filling line. The packaging for each product is almost identical, with minor size adjustments to accommodate bulk densities. The bulk densities within a product line vary considerably. The packaging department concentrates on filling each package to the correct weight and allowing the product volume in each package to float. All of the packages are premarked except for the product code and production series. The product code and series are printed on each filled package. The code and series are automatically stenciled with ink on the package as it passes through a roller pad.

The manufacturing unit has been successful in doubling the output of the packaging department with no significant capital spending. The packaging department work force was recently reduced to cut costs. Management does not believe the labor reduction will significantly impact the packaging unit operation efficiency.

The packaging unit was originally designed for half the current volume. Selected cost savings and productivity improvement projects account for the improved efficiency. The packaging line is semiautomated.

The product is classified as a specialty product with a high value added for the customer (one pound of the B.A. Team Industries' product could affect 1,000 pounds of the customers' finished product).

The warehouse department has been asked to check the packaging and containers while handling for storage and shipping. Everyone agrees that the packaging and containers need to be done right.

Several customers have complained that the product they received from the B.A. Team Industries was not properly marked such that the contents of the package could not be identified. This nonconformance did not meet the customers' requirements and violated safety rules. The customers returned the product and accepted replacement material. At least one customer threatened to go elsewhere for the product.

The quality business team added the nonconformance to the action item list (Exhibit A). The distribution action team was charged with the responsibility of taking action to prevent recurrence.

The action team constructed a flow chart (Exhibit B), cause-and-effect diagram (Exhibit C), and Pareto diagram (Exhibit D) as a team communication aid. The action team solved the problem using the PMSA problem-solving method (Exhibit F) and defined the cost of quality of the nonconformance (Exhibit E).

Exhibit A: Action Item List

SUBJECT	RESPONSIBILITY	BENEFIT	TARGET DATE
1. Goods returned due to improper identification (preventable).	Distribution — C.M. Ship Manufacturing — U.R. Wright	$158,000	July X, 19XX

Exhibit B: Simplified Flow Chart

PACKAGE LABELING SEQUENCE

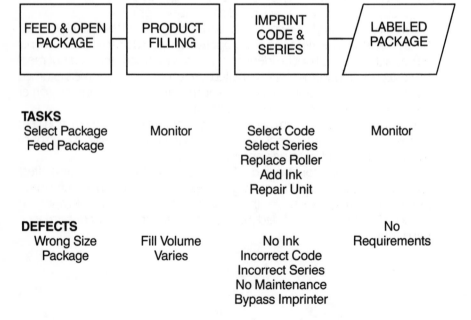

FEED & OPEN PACKAGE	PRODUCT FILLING	IMPRINT CODE & SERIES	LABELED PACKAGE

TASKS

Select Package Feed Package	Monitor	Select Code Select Series Replace Roller Add Ink Repair Unit	Monitor

DEFECTS

Wrong Size Package	Fill Volume Varies	No Ink Incorrect Code Incorrect Series No Maintenance Bypass Imprinter	No Requirements

Exhibit C: Cause-and-Effect Diagram

IMPROPER PACKAGE LABEL (Code & Series)

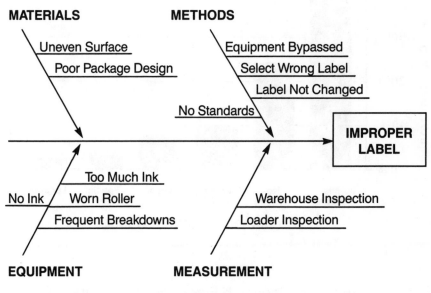

Cause Enumeration Type

Exhibit D: Pareto Chart

IMPROPER PACKAGE LABEL

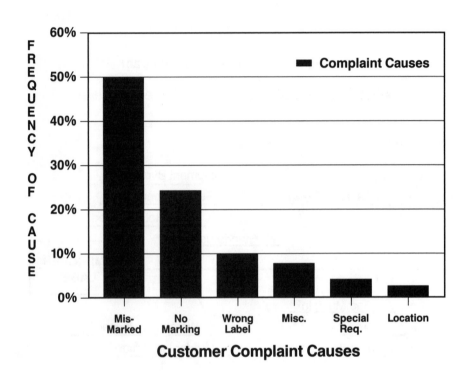

Complaint Causes & Frequency Summary

50% Code and series not complete or illegible
25% No code or series markings
10% Wrong code and/or series
8% Miscellaneous
4% Special customer requirement missing
3% Label in wrong location

Exhibit E: Benefits, Cost of Quality Calculation Sheet

The elimination of this defect (nonconformance) will result in the following benefits:

Source	$/Year

ORGANIZATIONAL BENEFITS:

1. Eliminate the occurrence of five complaints per year. (Cost to investigate and handle paperwork for a distribution complaint is $3,000.) $ 15,000

2. Eliminate the cost of return goods freight and handling. $ 10,000

3. Reduce working capital cost, storage cost, and handling of returned goods. Typically, returned goods are inventoried twice as long as good product before final disposition. $ 14,000

4. Eliminate business risk of customer claims due to inadvertent use of the wrong product (based on historical data). $ 50,000

5. Reduce internal warehouse appraisal and inspection cost for identification and field correction. $ 6,000

6. Cost to rework defective material. Cost based on actual outside toller (contractor) charges. $ 10,000

7. Reduce legal and regulatory risk of improperly marked packaged product being involved in a transportation incident or improper landfill disposal. $?

8. Maintenance cost reduction for repairing existing unreliable equipment (labor and materials). $ 3,000

Total Operating Cost Savings $108,000

9. Potential negative impact on sales revenue based on industry studies and marketing estimate. $ 50,000

Organization's Cost of Quality $158,000

CUSTOMER BENEFITS:

1. Eliminate cost of handling and returning complaint material.
2. Reduce the cost of inspecting incoming material.
3. Reduce the business risk of producing bad finished product.
4. Eliminate shutdown of production due to lack of correct material.
5. Reduce inventory cost by lowering reorder point.
6. Reduce business risk of complaints and claims by customers.

Exhibit F: PMSA Discussion

Problem Identification — Focus on Customer Requirements. Customers are receiving product that does not conform to mutually agreed upon requirements. The nonconformance is that product is being delivered that is not properly labeled (product code and series).

Measurement Focus Plan — Get the Facts. *(Data Collection Plan)* Investigate customer package marking complaints, list complaint causes, sort and plot data on Pareto chart (Exhibit D) for review, construct a flow chart (Exhibit B), and cause-and-effect diagram (Exhibit C) to aid action team communication and effectiveness (problem explanation and understanding).

(Root Cause) Seventy percent of complaints are caused by incomplete, illegible, or missing product code and/or series. *What would cause the markings not to be correct . . . the first time?*

1. Labeling equipment breaks down, but packing line keeps operating to meet schedule (pounds perceived to be more important than quality).
2. Labeling equipment breaks down and no one notices until several packages have been processed without the proper markings.
3. The packaging department has no specific standard or criteria for an acceptable package and container. The only two standards that are enforced are correct package weight and schedule maintenance.
4. Maintenance records show poor equipment reliability and performance for the existing process requirements.
5. Uneven and improper labeling results when there are wide variations in product bulk density (apparent package volume is not uniform). Note that this is not presently controllable.
6. No preventive maintenance program has been developed to minimize unscheduled downtime due to bearing failure, no ink, roller adjustment, etc.

(Conclusion) Labeling equipment does not conform to the requirements of the current process (system) and no acceptable/unacceptable package criteria have been defined for the department.

Solution(s) — Prevent Recurrence.

1. Define acceptable package performance criteria coupled with a formal inspection program and preventive maintenance.
    Comments: Does not eliminate the root cause, is costly, and labor-intensive.

2. Replace the packaging line with new equipment (filling, sealing, weighing, labeling, containerization, and wrapping).
    Comments: Too costly compared to identified savings and not necessary to solve the problem as defined. The identification of additional packaging problems might justify this solution.

3. Replace old labeling equipment with a system designed to conform to requirements (higher volume and bulk density variations) coupled with set criteria for acceptable packages and containers.
    Comments: Most economical, timely, and eliminates the root cause.

Action — Continuous Quality Improvement. Take action to prevent recurrence by implementation of the third solution alternative.

1. Implement new packaging standards and absorb short-term operating cost increases.

2. Justify expenditure for new labeling equipment (cost of quality). Seek approval as required.

3. Purchase/install/start up new system.

4. Monitor complaints and performance of new system.

[Result] Customer receives a package that conforms to requirements . . . the first time!

Summary

This example uses the PMSA method and common quality tools for solving the improper label problem. This method can be applied to any nonconformance of any existing system or operation. The solution was a modification of the packaging system to eliminate the root cause of the nonconformance. The new system is capable of meeting the process requirements all of the time.

Qualification of Suppliers

Factors/Criteria for the Most Confident Supplier

FACTORS	CRITERIA
1. Approved specifications/ requirements	The supplier and customer have documented, mutually agreed upon specifications/requirements.
2. Supplier quality survey	The supplier has completed and returned the quality survey.
3. Customer on-site visit	Customer quality team has evaluated the supplier's facility and process capability.
4. Statistical quality control	Supplier has implemented statistical quality control, and control charts are normally available for review.
5. Product certification	Supplier testing and certification are not required.
6. Customer testing	It is not necessary for the customer to test and approve incoming material.
7. Defective product/service	The supplier is responsible for defective materials and the cost impact on the customer.

American National Standards for Quality*

Standards for Auditing and Quality Systems

ANSI/ASQC Q1-1986. Generic Guidelines for Auditing of Quality Systems

The purpose of this standard is to provide the standard criteria and requirements for audit principles and the effective generic audit practices necessary to provide concerned management with the factual, objective information upon which to make decisions concerning its quality system adequacy and effectiveness.

ANSI/ASQC C1-1985 (ANSI Z1.8-1971). Specifications of General Requirements for a Quality Program

This standard was designed to provide a description of the basic principles essential to the assurance of quality. It is intended to be imposed internally by management and externally through both sales and purchase contracts. Broad use of this standard is intended to minimize the number of nonstandard and conflicting quality requirements that otherwise will be found in sales and purchasing contracts.

ANSI/ASQC Q90-1987. Quality Management and Quality Assurance Standards — Guidelines for Selection and Use

The purposes of this American National Standard are as follows: a) to clarify the distinctions and interrelationships among the principle quality concepts, and b) to provide guidelines for the selection and use of a series of standards on quality systems that can be used for internal quality management purposes (Q94) and for external quality assurance purposes (Q91, Q92, and Q93).

ANSI/ASQC Q91-1987. Quality Systems — Model for Quality Assurance in Design/Development, Production, Installation, and Servicing

Use Q91 when conformance to specified requirements is to be assured by the supplier during several stages which may include design/development, production, installation, and servicing.

ANSI/ASQC Q92-1987. Quality Systems — Model for Quality Assurance in Production and Installation

Use Q92 when conformance to specified requirements is to be assured by the supplier during production and installation.

---

*Published by ASQC

ANSI/ASQC Q93-1987. Quality Systems — Model for Quality Assurance in Final Inspection and Test

This standard should be used when conformance to specified requirements is to be assured by the supplier solely at final inspection and test.

ANSI/ASQC Q94-1987. Quality Management and Quality System Elements — Guidelines

This standard describes a basic set of elements by which quality management systems can be developed and implemented.

A QUALITY MASTER PLAN SCHEDULE

OVERVIEW

GANTT CHART

MODIFIED CRITICAL PATH DIAGRAM

ACTIVITY RESOURCE REPORT

Overview

The quality master plan schedule is an overview of the activities required for implementation of total quality management for an organization. Although the major target groups are identified, for the schedule to be meaningful the size and dimension of the organization must be known.

The schedule (template) gives a view of the resources and extent of the transition required for quality management. The schedule is in the same format as the quality master plan [i.e., divided into goals/strategies and activities (steps)].

The Schedule When an iterative approach to planning is used, the schedule template can serve as a rough first cut that can be refined later. Since not everything can be planned in detail on the first pass, concentrate on the short-term activities. You are encouraged to use the schedule template to formulate the requirements for your quality plan.

The template names (tongue-in-cheek) the groups involved in the process as if they were one individual [i.e., E.X. Envision (EXE), M.G. Talented (MGT), B.A. Team (BAT)], and quality assurance coordinator (QAC). In reality, there could be several departments or functions that will be trained at different times and locations. The implementation of the quality process involves everyone, not just the quality professionals.

There are 48 activities scheduled to be completed over 32 months. However, no individual time constraints have been imposed. The effort is estimated on a direct labor per task basis and does not include development or instructor time. The total effort for the quality assurance coordinator depends on the use of outside resources and the size of the organization.

The critical path shows that the process can be initialized within six months and results will be realized within eight months.

The following schedules are included in the quality master plan:

1. Gantt chart.
2. Critical path diagram.
3. Activity resource report.

GANTT CHART

PROJECT: QUALITY MASTER PLAN

GOAL/STRATEGY/ACTIVITY	YEAR ONE Jan	Feb	Mar	Apr	May	Jun	Jul	Aug	Sep	Oct	Nov	Dec	YEAR TWO Jan	Feb	Mar	Apr
I. INTEGRATE & PROMOTE QUALITY MANAGEMENT																
A. COMMIT TO A QUALITY POLICY																
1. Evaluate Policies	≡															
2. Define Policy Requirements	≡															
3. Draft Policy & Circulate	≡															
4. Publish Policy*	C≡															
B. MARKET TOTAL QUALITY & TEAM BUILDING																
1. Plan Promotion Campaign Events	≡≡≡≡≡															
2. Select Media		≡														
C. DEMONSTRATE MANAGEMENT COMMITMENT																
1/2. Lead Teams & Complete Education		════════		═ ongoing ═									══════			═
3. Advocate Quality & Support Champions		════════		═ ongoing ═									══════			═
D. INVOLVE ALL LEVELS																
1. Define Criteria for Involvement		≡≡														
2. Conduct Periodic Assessment								═════════		═ ongoing ═					═	
II. BUILD A RESPONSIVE ORGANIZATION TO CUSTOMER NEEDS																
A. INTEGRATE QUALITY INTO THE BUSINESS																
1. Appoint Quality Coordinator	≡≡≡≡															
2. Establish a Quality Management Team	≡≡≡															
3. Form Quality Business Team(s)	≡≡≡≡≡≡≡															
4. Organize Quality Action Teams*		≡≡≡≡≡≡≡														
B. QUALITY EDUCATION																
1/2. Plan & Develop Education Strategies	≡≡≡≡≡≡≡															
3. Quality Management Seminar		≡≡≡≡≡≡≡														
4. Quality Awareness Education*				C≡≡≡≡≡≡≡≡												
5. Quality Action Skills Education							═════════									
6. Quality Process Implementation Methods												═════════				═

Note: *Indicates milestone

117

GOAL/STRATEGY/ACTIVITY	YEAR ONE Jan–Dec	YEAR TWO Jan–Apr
III. CONSISTENTLY PROVIDE VALUE TO CUSTOMER		
A. BUILD A FOUNDATION FOR IMPROVEMENT		
1. Initialize the Process*	C========== (Jun onward)	========
2. Develop Action Item List	C===== (Jun–Jul)	
3. Publish Quality Action Plan*	======= (Jul–Aug)	
4. Identify Customer/Supplier Requirement		=================
5. Develop Outreach Program		=====
6. Customer CPR Program*	==================== (Jun–Sep)	
B. APPLY QUALITY TECHNIQUES & PREVENTION TOOLS		
1. Problem Definition	C============ongoing============	=======
2. Measurement Focus	C===========ongoing===========	=======
3. Solution	C=========== ongoing =========	=======
4. Action*	C========== ongoing =========	======
C. IMPLEMENT SQC METHODS		
1. Select a SQC Method	================ (Sep–Nov)	
2. Implement SQC Pilot Process*		=================
3. Expand SQC to Remaining Operations		
4. Process In Control & Make Capable*		============
5. Qualify Suppliers*		===.
IV. ACHIEVE CONTINUOUS IMPROVEMENT		
A. ESTABLISH A QUALITY EDUCATION SYSTEM		
1. Ongoing/Routine Education		
2. New Employee Orientation		
3. Integrated Training		
B. FORM AUDIT SYSTEMS		
1. Internal Audits		
2. Self-Audits		
3. Supplier Audits		
C. INTEGRATE TOTAL PREVENTION		
1. Prevention Methods (DEVSA)		====== ongoing ==
D. INTEGRATE QUALITY MANAGEMENT		
1. Organizational Structure		
2. Evaluate Job Description/Performance		
3. Customer Feedback		
4. Review Procedures		
5. Annual Quality Management Plan		====== ongoing ===

Note: *Indicates milestone

GOAL/STRATEGY/ACTIVITY		YEAR ONE												YEAR TWO			
		Jan	Feb	Mar	Apr	May	Jun	Jul	Aug	Sep	Oct	Nov	Dec	Jan	Feb	Mar	Apr
RESOURCE GROUP SUMMARY																	
E.X. Envision	work days/month	6	4	2	1	1	1	1	2	2	2	2	1	2	1	2	1
M.G. Talented		2	6	2	2	3	4	6	7	5	5	5	4	5	15	6	5
Q.A. Coordinator		8	7	6	3	3	2	2	3	2	2	1	3	4	3	4	3
BA Team					1	3	3	4	3	2	1	2	5	5	5	7	5
UNASSIGNED																	
TOTAL DAYS		16	17	10	7	10	10	13	15	11	10	10	13	16	24	19	14

119

GOAL/STRATEGY/ACTIVITY	YEAR TWO								YEAR THREE							
	May	Jun	Jul	Aug	Sep	Oct	Nov	Dec	Jan	Feb	Mar	Apr	May	Jun	Jul	Aug
I. INTEGRATE & PROMOTE QUALITY MANAGEMENT																
A. COMMIT TO A QUALITY POLICY																
1. Evaluate Policies																
2. Define Policy Requirements																
3. Draft Policy & Circulate																
4. Publish Policy*																
B. MARKET TOTAL QUALITY & TEAM BUILDING																
1. Plan Promotion Campaign Events																
2. Select Media																
C. DEMONSTRATE MANAGEMENT COMMITMENT																
1/2. Lead Teams & Complete Education																
3. Advocate Quality & Support Champions																
D. INVOLVE ALL LEVELS																
1. Define Criteria for Involvement																
2. Conduct Periodic Assessment																
II. BUILD A RESPONSIVE ORGANIZATION TO CUSTOMER NEEDS																
A. INTEGRATE QUALITY INTO THE BUSINESS																
1. Appoint Quality Coordinator																
2. Establish a Quality Management Team																
3. Form Quality Business Team(s)																
4. Organize Quality Action Teams*																
B. QUALITY EDUCATION																
1/2. Plan & Develop Education Strategies																
3. Quality Management Seminar																
4. Quality Awareness Education*																
5. Quality Action Skills Education																
6. Quality Process Implementation Methods																

Note: *Indicates milestone

GOAL/STRATEGY/ACTIVITY	YEAR TWO								YEAR THREE							
	May	Jun	Jul	Aug	Sep	Oct	Nov	Dec	Jan	Feb	Mar	Apr	May	Jun	Jul	Aug
III. CONSISTENTLY PROVIDE VALUE TO CUSTOMER																
A. BUILD A FOUNDATION FOR IMPROVEMENT																
1. Initialize the Process*	■															
2. Develop Action Item List																
3. Publish Quality Action Plan*																
4. Identify Customer/Supplier Requirement																
5. Develop Outreach Program	■	■	■	■	■	■	■									
6. Customer CPR Program*																
B. APPLY QUALITY TECHNIIQUES & PREVENTION TOOLS																
1. Problem Definition	■	■	■	■	■	■	■	■	■	■	■	■	■	■	■	■
2. Measurement Focus	■	■	■	■	■	■	■	■	■	■	■	■	■	■	■	■
3. Solution	■	■	■	■	■	■	■	■	■	■	■	■	■	■	■	■
4. Action*	■	■	■	■	■	■	■	■	■	■	■	■	■	■	■	■
C. IMPLEMENT SQC METHODS																
1. Select a SQC Method																
2. Implement SQC Pilot Process*																
3. Expand SQC to Remaining Operations			■	■	■	■	■	■	■	■	■	■	■	■	■	■
4. Process In Control & Make Capable*	■	■	■	■	■	■	■	■	■	■	■	■	■	■	■	■
5. Qualify Suppliers*																
IV. ACHIEVE CONTINUOUS IMPROVEMENT																
A. ESTABLISH A QUALITY EDUCATION SYSTEM																
1. Ongoing/Routine Education			■	■	■	■	■	■	■	■	■	■	■	■	■	■
2. New Employee Orientation			■	■	■	■	■	■	■	■	■	■	■	■	■	■
3. Integrated Training			■	■	■	■	■	■	■	■	■	■	■	■	■	■
B. FORM AUDIT SYSTEMS																
1. Internal Audits									■	■	■	■	■	■	■	■
2. Self-Audits											■	■	■	■	■	■
3. Supplier Audits												■	■	■	■	■
C. INTEGRATE TOTAL PREVENTION																
1. Prevention Methods (DEVSA)	■	■	■	■	■	■	■	■	■	■	■	■	■	■	■	■
D. INTEGRATE QUALITY MANAGEMENT																
1. Organizational Structure									■	■	■	■	■	■		
2. Evaluate Job Description/Performance									■	■	■	■	■	■	■	
3. Customer Feedback									■	■	■	■	■	■		
4. Review Procedures												■	■	■	■	■
5. Annual Quality Management Plan	■	■	■	■	■	■	■	■	■	■	■	■	■	■	■	■

Note: *Indicates milestone

GOAL/STRATEGY/ACTIVITY		YEAR TWO								YEAR THREE							
		May	Jun	Jul	Aug	Sep	Oct	Nov	Dec	Jan	Feb	Mar	Apr	May	Jun	Jul	Aug
RESOURCE GROUP SUMMARY																	
E.X. Envision	work days/month	2	1	2	2	2	5	6	5	6	5	5	5	5	4	2	2
M.G. Talented		6	5	6	7	6	7	7	7	8	7	11	11	12	10	10	7
Q.A. Coordinator		3	3	3	4	4	4	4	4	5	5	6	7	6	5	5	5
BA Team		6	5	6	6	5	3	2	2	2	2	2	2	3	2	2	2
UNASSIGNED																	
TOTAL DAYS		17	14	17	19	17	19	19	18	21	19	24	25	26	21	19	16

MODIFIED CRITICAL PATH DIAGRAM

QUALITY MASTER PLAN

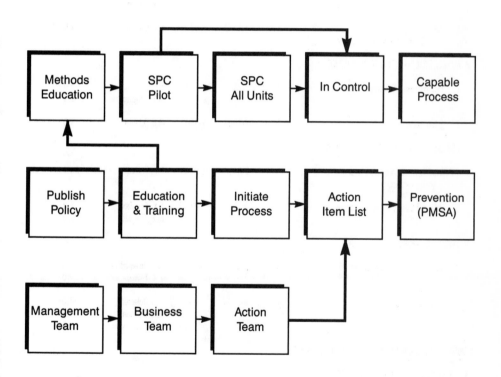

QUALITY MASTER PLAN — ACTIVITY RESOURCE REPORT

--------------------NAME--------------------	BUS DAYS	START	END	--------WHO--------	DAYS
I. INTEGRATE & PROMOTE QUALITY MANAGEMENT					
A. COMMIT TO A QUALITY POLICY					
1. Evaluate Policies	3	1-02-Y1	1-04-Y1	E.X. Envision	1.0
				Q.A. Coordinator	2.0
2. Define Policy Requirements	6	1-09-Y1	1-16-Y1	E.X. Envision	1.0
				Q.A. Coordinator	1.0
3. Draft Policy & Circulate	7	1-16-Y1	1-24-Y1	E.X. Envision	1.0
				Q.A. Coordinator	1.0
4. Publish Policy* – Quality Policy or Mission Statement	5	1-23-Y1	1-27-Y1	E.X. Envision	1.0
B. MARKET TOTAL QUALITY & TEAM BUILDING					
1. Plan Promotion Campaign Events	21	1-23-Y1	2-20-Y1	E.X. Envision	1.0
				M.G. Talented	4.0
2. Select Media	5	2-20-Y1	2-24-Y1	M.G. Talented	1.0
C. DEMONSTRATE MANAGEMENT COMMITMENT					
1/2. Lead Teams & Complete Education – Quality Certificate	750	2-06-Y1	12-20-Y1	E.X. Envision	36.0
3. Advocate Quality & Support Champions	744	2-27-Y1	1-02-Y3	E.X. Envision	9.0
				M.G. Talented	2.0
D. INVOLVE ALL LEVELS					
1. Define Criteria for Involvement	10	2-06-Y1	2-17-Y1	M.G. Talented	2.0
				E.X. Envision	1.0
2. Conduct Periodic Assessment	750	6-26-Y1	5-08-Y3	M.G. Talented	12.0
				E.X. Envision	4.0
				Q.A. Coordinator	6.0
II. BUILD A RESPONSIVE ORGANIZATION TO CUSTOMER NEEDS					
A. INTEGRATE QUALITY INTO THE BUSINESS					
1. Appoint Quality Coordinator – Quality Assurance Coordinator	20	1-02-Y1	1-27-Y1	E.X. Envision	1.0
2. Establish a Quality Management Team	11	1-23-Y1	2-06-Y1	Q.A. Coordinator	3.0
				E.X. Envision	1.0
3. Form Quality Business Team(s) – Quality Business Teams	35	2-06-Y1	3-24-Y1	Q.A. Coordinator	5.0
				E.X. Envision	1.0

Note: *Indicates milestone

QUALITY MASTER PLAN — ACTIVITY RESOURCE REPORT

--------------------NAME--------------------	BUS DAYS	START	END	-------WHO-------	DAYS
4. Organize Quality Action Teams* – Action Teams Initialized	46	3-13-Y1	5-15-Y1	Q.A. Coordinator M.G. Talented	3.0 1.0
B. QUALITY EDUCATION					
1/2. Plan & Develop Education Strategies – Quality Education Plan	45	1-23-Y1	3-24-Y1	E.X. Envision M.G. Talented Q.A. Coordinator	1.0 2.0 7.0
3. Quality Management Seminar – Certificate	46	3-13-Y1	5-15-Y1	M.G. Talented Q.A. Coordinator	2.0 2.0
4. Quality Awareness Education* – Quality Certificate	88	4-10-Y1	8-09-Y1	M.G. Talented BA Team Q.A. Coordinator	3.0 5.0 3.0
5. Quality Action Skills Education	56	9-04-Y1	11-20-Y1	M.G. Talented E.X. Envision Q.A. Coordinator	2.0 2.0 2.0
6. Quality Process Implementation Methods	262	12-04-Y1	12-04-Y2	M.G. Talented BA Team Q.A. Coordinator	2.0 1.0 2.0
III. CONSISTENTLY PROVIDE VALUE TO CUSTOMER					
A. BUILD A FOUNDATION FOR IMPROVEMENT					
1. Initialize the Process* – Problem List	261	5-15-Y1	5-14-Y2	M.G. Talented BA Team	2.0 2.0
2. Develop Action Item List – Action Item List	45	6-12-Y1	8-11-Y1	M.G. Talented BA Team	3.0 1.0
3. Publish Quality Action Plan* – Quality Action Plan	35	7-10-Y1	8-25-Y1	M.G. Talented	2.0
4. Identify Customer/Supplier Requirements – Verification of Requirements	90	11-27-Y1	3-30-Y2	Q.A. Coordinator M.G. Talented BA Team	3.0 3.0 10.0
5. Develop Outreach Program – Customer Profile	140	3-20-Y2	10-01-Y2	M.G. Talented Q.A. Coordinator BA Team	15.0 10.0 25.0
6. Customer CPR Program* – Customer CPR Program	108	5-01-Y1	9-27-Y1	Q.A. Coordinator M.G. Talented BA Team	5.0 5.0 5.0
B. APPLY QUALITY TECHNIQUES & PREVENTION TOOLS					
1. Problem Definition – State Problems	689	5-15-Y1	1-02-Y3	M.G. Talented BA Team	10.0 10.0
2. Measurement Focus – Root Cause Defined	668	6-12-Y1	1-01-Y3	M.G. Talented BA Team	10.0 10.0

Note: *Indicates milestone

QUALITY MASTER PLAN — ACTIVITY RESOURCE REPORT

--------------------NAME--------------------	BUS DAYS	START	END	-------WHO-------	DAYS
3. Solution	646	7-10-Y1	12-30-Y3	M.G. Talented	20.0
– Alternative Solutions				BA Team	10.0
4. Action	634	7-31-Y1	1-02-Y3	M.G. Talented	10.0
– Prevent Recurrence				BA Team	2.0
C. IMPLEMENT SQC METHODS					
1. Select a SQC Method	85	8-01-Y1	11-27-Y1	M.G. Talented	7.0
				Q.A. Coordinator	3.0
2. Implement SQC Pilot Process*	90	11-27-Y1	3-30-Y2	Q.A. Coordinator	5.0
– Pilot SPC Program Success				M.G. Talented	5.0
				BA Team	5.0
3. Expand SQC to Remaining Operations	374	7-30-Y2	1-02-Y3	M.G. Talented	12.0
– All Processes on SPC				Q.A. Coordinator	12.0
4. Process In Control & Make Capable*	494	2-12-Y2	1-02-Y3	M.G. Talented	6.0
– In Control/Stable Process				BA Team	12.0
5. Qualify Suppliers*	10	2-01-Y2	8-14-Y2	M.G. Talented	10.0
– Suppliers Approved					
IV. ACHIEVE CONTINUOUS IMPROVEMENT					
A. ESTABLISH A QUALITY EDUCATION SYSTEM					
1. Ongoing/Routine Education	374	7-30-Y2	1-02-Y3	M.G. Talented	2.2
– Quality Training Course				Q.A. Coordinator	4.4
				E.X. Envision	2.2
				BA Team	2.2
2. New Employee Orientation	374	7-30-Y2	1-02-Y3	Q.A. Coordinator	2.0
– New Employee Certification				M.G. Talented	1.0
3. Integrated Training	374	7-30-Y2	1-02-Y3	E.X. Envision	2.2
– All Meetings Include Quality				M.G. Talented	2.2
B. FORM AUDIT SYSTEMS					
1. Internal Audits	262	12-31-Y2	12-31-Y3	Q.A. Coordinator	12.0
– Audit Report & Rating				M.G. Talented	4.0
2. Self Audits	179	2-22-Y3	10-30-Y3	M.G. Talented	1.0
– Audit Report & Assessment				Q.A. Coordinator	5.0
3. Supplier Audits	127	3-29-Y3	9-23-Y3	M.G. Talented	1.0
– Completed Supplier Preaudit				Q.A. Coordinator	3.0
C. INTEGRATE TOTAL PREVENTION					
1. Prevention Methods	523	1-01-Y2	1-01-Y3	M.G. Talented	5.0
				BA Team	5.0
				Q.A. Coordinator	3.0

Note: *Indicates milestone

QUALITY MASTER PLAN — ACTIVITY RESOURCE REPORT

--------------------NAME--------------------	BUS DAYS	START	END	-------WHO-------	DAYS
D. INTEGRATE QUALITY MANAGEMENT					
1. Organizational Structure – Quality Organization Formed	196	9-27-Y2	6-27-Y3	E.X. Envision	20.0
2. Evaluate Job Description/Performance	196	10-19-Y2	7-19-Y3	E.X. Envision M.G. Talented Q.A. Coordinator	7.0 20.0 3.0
3. Customer Feedback –Ongoing Customer Feedback	196	9-28-Y2	6-28-Y3	E.X. Envision M.G. Talented Q.A. Coordinator	3.0 10.0 10.0
4. Review Procedures –Customer Focused Procedures	196	3-04-Y3	12-02-Y3	M.G. Talented Q.A. Coordinator BA Team	30.0 3.0 5.0
5. Annual Quality Management Plan –Quality Business Plan	526	12-25-Y1	12-30-Y3	E.X. Envision M.G. Talented Q.A. Coordinator	2.0 10.0 20.0
TOTAL PROJECT		1-02-Y1	5-08-Y4		587.4

RESOURCE GROUP SUMMARY

		START	END	WHO	DAYS
E.X. Envision		1-02-Y1	12-30-Y3	EXE	97.4
M.G. Talented		1-23-Y1	12-30-Y3	MGT	239.4
Q.A. Coordinator		1-02-Y1	12-30-Y3	QAC	140.4
BA Team		4-10-Y1	12-30-Y3	BAT	110.2
TOTAL PROJECT		1-02-Y1	12-30-Y3		587.4

GLOSSARY

Action Item List: A list of problems or defects with assigned responsibility and target date for completion.

Action Team: A group of people assigned to solve problems by measuring, defining root-cause solutions and taking action.

Appraisal: Inspecting and checking of outputs of any work activity and or process.

Audit: Inspection and examination of a process or quality system to ensure compliance to requirements. Audits can apply to an entire company or be specific to a function or production step. The most common audits are good manufacturing practice (GMP), good laboratory practice (GLP), quality systems audit, and product specific process audits.

Average: Sum of a group of numbers divided by the number of numbers in the group; indicates process level being achieved.

Brainstorming: A form of creative thinking in which ideas about a particular topic are solicited in a nonjudgmental, unrestricted manner from all members of a group.

Cause-and-Effect (Fishbone) Diagram: A graphic way of identifying and sorting possible causes of a problem.

Center Line: Represents overall operating level of the process.

Chart: Display of information in graphic form.

Conformance: When the inputs and outputs of a process consistently meet specific and measurable requirements the first time.

Control: Keeping something within the boundaries; making something behave in a desired, predetermined way.

Control Chart: Special type of graph depicting the natural capabilities of the process.

Control Limits: Defines natural boundaries of a process within specified confidence levels.

Conventional Wisdom: A subjective attitude that allows errors in products and services delivered to customers. The traditional approach to working toward quality which has proven to be ineffective.

Corrective Action: Documented and purposeful change implemented to eliminate a specific cause of an identified defect or nonconformance.

Cost of Quality: The price of doing it wrong (costs of not conforming to requirements) and the price of inspecting and checking (cost of procedures, appraisal, and compliance) added together.

Customer: Receiver or user of outputs (products, services, or information) from your work group process. The customer can be an individual or company, internal or external.

DEVSA: Prevention techniques for the development of new systems or processes right the first time. The prevention steps are: Define, Evaluate, Validate, Systematize, Action.

DOE (Design of Experiments): A statistical tool used to discover key variables in product and process design to reduce variations. Founded by Sir Ronald Fisher of Great Britain.

Expectations: The needs and wants of a customer. The definition implies a certain anticipation or prospects of the future.

Factor: A value by which to multiply or divide.

Fishbone: *(See Cause-and-Effect Diagram)*

Graphs (Trend Charts): Tools for organization and summarization to aid in the analysis of data. Trend is a continued rise or fall in a series of points.

Histogram: Plots the frequency of each particular measurement in a group of measurements (a bar graph that depicts a frequency distribution).

In Control: Stable pattern of behavior in a process.

Operation: A single step in a process.

Out of Control: Unstable or nonrandom behavior in a process.

Paradigm: An outstandingly clear or typical example.

Paradigm Process: An outstandingly clear or typical example of a series of steps or operations that lead to a desired result.

Pareto Chart: A tool for ranking or prioritizing data thereby isolating the vital few from the trivial many.

Performance Standard: Expectation of how often a job or task should be done right according to requirements and specifications.

PMSA (Problem, Measurement, Solution, Action): Problem-solving techniques preventing recurrence of defects or problems of existing systems or processes. The problem-solving steps are: problem, measurement, solution, action.

Precontrol: A simplified method for control charting with narrow upper and lower control limits.

Prevention: Causing nonconformances and errors not to happen.

Price of Conformance: What it costs to get things done right the first time.

Price of Nonconformance: What it costs to do things wrong; resulting in losses (i.e., money, time, opportunity).

Process: Set or series of conditions or causes, working together to produce a desired result.

Process Evaluation: An information-gathering tool to use with any work activity. It breaks down the job into component parts (inputs and outputs) and establishes requirements for each part (validation/knowledge/equipment/procedures).

Quality: What a product or service (output) that consistently meets requirements, expectations, and provides value (or utility) to the customer (recipient or receiver) has.

Quality Policy: A management statement that enables everyone in a company to know where management stands on quality.

Quality Triad: A holistic focus for defining quality whose components are conforming to requirements, striving to meet expectations, and maximizing value (utility).

Range: Calculated as the largest minus smallest in a group of numbers; used as an estimate of the variability in the process.

Requirement: The customer's needs and wants for a particular product or service. Implies a certain necessity or condition for a current or existing situation.

Root Cause: Original reason(s) for not meeting requirements within a process. When removed, the nonconformance or defect will be eliminated.

Run: Sequence of seven points all above the center line or all below the center of a control chart; indicates nonrandom behavior.

Sample: Measurement of a particular parameter or property.

Sample Size: Number of observations within a subgroup.

Scope: Clearly identifying and defining the process to its narrowest form. If the scope is changed, so are the inputs and outputs.

Statistical: Application of math principles for the evaluation of numbers or data.

Statistical Quality Control (SQC): The application of statistics for the control of process or systems.

Supplier: A company or individual who provides input to jobs, whether from inside the company or external to it. In quality improvement, the customer/supplier relationship becomes an interactive relationship that calls for sharing requirements and expectations.

System: A series of steps taken to ensure that a stated goal is achieved.

Trend: Sequence of seven points all increasing or decreasing; indicates nonrandom behavior.

Zero Defects: The attitude of defect prevention through understanding and meeting the requirements of a job or task all the time.

BIBLIOGRAPHY

ANSI/ASQC Q1-1986. *Generic Guidelines for Auditing of Quality Systems.* Milwaukee: American Society for Quality Control, 1986.

ANSI/ASQC Q94-1987. *Quality Management and Quality Systems Elements — Guidelines.* Milwaukee: American Society for Quality Control, 1987.

ASQC Chemical and Process Industries Division, Chemical Interest Committee. *Quality Assurance for the Chemical and Process Industries — A Manual of Good Practices.* Milwaukee: American Society for Quality Control, 1988.

Crosby, Philip B. *Quality Without Tears.* New York: McGraw-Hill Book Company, 1984.

Shea, Gordon. "Building Trust in the Work Place." *AMA Review* No. 2309. New York: American Management Association, 1984.

BIBLIOGRAPHY

SUGGESTED READING

ANSI/ASQC Q90-1987 Series. *Quality Management and Quality Assurance Standards.* Milwaukee: American Society for Quality Control, 1987.

Badger, Morton E. *Practical Quality Management in the Chemical Process Industry.* New York: American Management Association, 1988.

Bhote, Keki R. *World Class Quality.* New York: American Management Association, 1988.

Box, G.E.P., and N.R. Draper. *Evolutionary Operations.* New York: John Wiley & Sons, 1969.

Box, G.E.P., W. G. Hunter, and J.S. Hunter. *Statistics for Experimenters.* New York: John Wiley & Sons, 1978.

Burr, Irving W. *Elementary Statistical Quality Control.* New York: Marcel Dekker, 1979.

Crosby, Philip B. *Quality Is Free.* New York: McGraw-Hill Book Company, 1979.

Crosby, Philip B., *Quality Without Tears.* New York: McGraw-Hill Book Company, 1984.

Deming, W. Edwards. *Out of the Crisis.* Cambridge: Massachusetts Institute of Technology, Center for Advanced Engineering Study, 1986.

Deming, W. Edwards. *Quality Productivity, and Competitive Position.* Cambridge: Massachusetts Institute of Technology, Center for Advanced Engineering Study, 1982.

Diamond, William J. *Practical Experiment Designs for Engineers and Scientists.* 1981, Belmont, CA: Lifetime Learning Publications, 1981.

Enrick, Norbert L. *Manufacturing Analysis for Productivity and Quality/Cost Enhancement,* 2nd ed. New York: Industrial Press Incorporated, 1983.

Feigenbaum, Armand V. *Total Quality Control.* New York: McGraw-Hill Book Company, 1983.

Gitlow, Howard S., and Shirley J. Gitlow. *The Deming Guide to Quality and Competitive Position.* Englewood Cliffs, NJ: Prentice Hall, 1986.

Grant, Eugene L., and Richard S. Leavenworth. *Statistical Quality Control,* 6th ed. New York: McGraw-Hill Book Company, 1980.

Guaspari, John. *I Know It When I See It.* New York: AMACOM, 1985.

Ishikawa, Kaoru. *Guide to Quality Control,* 2nd ed. White Plains, NY: Kraus International Publications, 1982.

Juran, J.M. *Juran on Planning for Quality.* New York: The Free Press, 1988.

Juran, J.M. *Quality Control Handbook,* 4th ed. New York: McGraw-Hill Book Company, 1988.

Ott, Ellis R. *Process Quality Control: Troubleshooting and Interpretation of Data.* New York: McGraw-Hill Book Company, 1975.

Russell, J.P. *Quality Management Assessment Checklist.* Allentown, PA: J.P. Russell & Associates, 1989.

Scherkenbach, William W. *The Deming Route to Quality and Productivity: Road Maps and Roadblocks.* Rockville, MD: Mercury Press/Fairchild Publications, 1986.

Waterman, Robert H. Jr. *The Renewal Factor.* New York: Bantam Books, Inc., 1987.

Videotapes

Conway, Bill. *The Right Way to Manage.* Nashua, NH: Conway Quality Inc., 1983.

Crosby, Philip B. *Quality Is Free.* Winter Park, FL: Philip Crosby Associates, 1984.

Deming, W Edwards. *Management's Five Deadly Diseases.* Chicago: Encyclopedia Britannica, 1984.

INDEX